Bob

Second Acts

Also by Stephen M. Pollan and Mark Levine

Die Broke
Live Rich
The Die Broke Complete Book of Money
The Die Broke Financial Problem Solver

Second Acts

*Creating the Life
You Really Want,
Building the Career
You Truly Desire*

STEPHEN M. POLLAN
and
MARK LEVINE

Quill
A HarperResource Book
An Imprint of HarperCollinsPublishers

Dedication

To Robert Pollan and Freda Levine
whose Second Acts continue to inspire.

HarperCollins books may be purchased for educational, business, or sales promotional use. For information please write: Special Markets Department, HarperCollins Publishers Inc., 10 East 53rd Street, New York, NY 10022.

First HarperResource/Quill paperback edition published 2004

Designed by Pete Lippincott, D&G Limited, LLC

The Library of Congress has catalogued the hardcover edition as follows:
Pollan, Stephen M.
   Second acts : creating the life you really want, building the career you truly desire / Stephen M. Pollan and Mark Levine.
      p. cm.
   Includes Index
   ISBN 0-06-051487-6
1. Career changes. 2. Career development. 3. Self-actualization (psychology) I. Levine, Mark, 1958- II. Title

HF5384.P648 2003
650.14—dc21   2002032928

ISBN 0-06-051488-4 (pbk.)

04 05 06 07 08   RRD   10 9 8 7 6 5 4 3 2 1

Contents

Acknowledgments

The authors would like to thank Ambrose Bierce, Tony Blair, Kathleen A. Brehony, Lydia Bronte, Italo Calvino, Joseph Campbell, Charles Horton Cooley, Calvin Coolidge, Aleister Crowley, Benjamin Disraeli, Peter Drucker, David Elkind, F. Scott Fitzgerald, Benjamin Franklin, John Kenneth Galbraith, Shakti Gawain, Mark Gerzon, Louise Hart, Hillel, John Lennon, Stella Terrill Mann, Stephanie Marston, Groucho Marx, Ronald S. Miller, Anais Nin, Alexandra Robbins, John C. Robinson, Seneca, Zalman Schacter-Shalomi, Sophocles, Robert Louis Stevenson, Henry David Thoreau, John Updike, Abby Wilner, Margaret Young, and Rabbi Zusya of Hanipol whose words and writings stirred our own thoughts and imaginations.

Thanks to Sherwood Anderson, Brigitte Bardot, Roseanne Barr, Sonny Bono, Jimmy Carter, James Carville, Tom Clancy, Hillary Rodham Clinton, George Foreman, Michael J. Fox, Paul Gauguin, Ulysses S. Grant, Ron Howard, Glenda Jackson, Steve Jobs, Michael Jordan, Jack Kemp, Ray Kroc, John le Carré, John Mahoney, Jackie Mason, Melina Mercouri, Michael Milken, Heather Mills, Grandma Moses, Ronald Reagan, J. K. Rowling, Harlan Sanders, John Tesh, Harry S Truman, Steven Van Zandt, and Jesse Ventura, whose very public Second Acts helped inspire other, more private but no less remarkable Second Acts.

Thanks also to Marilyn Abraham, Betsy Berg, David Bowman, Dr. Roger Brunswick, Sean Cassidy, Gina Garrubbo, John Jacobsen, Dale Klamfoth, Erik Kolbell, Mitchell Kossof, Sandy MacGregor, Jane Morrow, David Newman, Charles Sodikoff, and Arthur Taylor for their advice and input.

Thanks to the clients of Stephen M. Pollan for letting us draw on and share their thoughts, fears, problems, and triumphs.

Thanks to Dave Conti and Megan Newman of HarperCollins for their enthusiasm and guidance in our own Second Act.

Thanks to our agent, Stuart Krichevsky, for his continued confidence and support in helping us in our never-ending process of reinvention.

Finally, thanks to our wives, Corky Pollan and Deirdre Martin Levine, for being the real stars in our lives.

How to Use This Book

This book is a guide to reinventing your life. Its goal is to help you launch, what I call, your Second Act. That's the life you've always dreamed of leading, but until now have, for one reason or another, been unable to achieve. It doesn't matter whether your Second Act involves a change of career, relocation, parenthood, or entrepreneurship. The program I outline in these pages will help you finally live out your dream.

The first part of the book should be read in its entirety. It briefly explains my ideas about Second Acts and then quickly moves on to help you develop the kind of attitude you'll need to succeed. Along the way, through the use of some simple exercises, it will help you flesh out your ideas and make hopes and dreams real. It will also help you determine the hurdles you may need to overcome along the way.

Part 2 provides advice and techniques for overcoming each of the 12 types of barriers you're apt to uncover and encounter. Like Part 1, it contains exercises designed to give you the tools you'll need to overcome any and every obstacle you'll face. In this instance, however, you'll need to read only the chapters relevant to your particular Second Act. Of course, reading them all wouldn't hurt and might even help.

Finally, Part 3 offers advice on pulling all the elements together into a cohesive and comprehensive script for your Second Act; a checklist that will take you step by step from where you are today to the moment when you're living the life of your dreams. It also offers my thoughts about why reinventing your life need not be a once in a lifetime process.

The journey on which you're about to embark isn't easy. You'll need to do some potentially painful self analysis and some time-consuming research to reach your goal. But, climbing to a incredible summit is always work. And I promise you, the pay off will be transcendent. Self reinvention is a glorious and empowering adventure. I envy you.

Introduction to the Paperback Edition

"There has never been a better time to launch your Second Act." When I wrote that sentence a year ago in the first edition of this book, and when I repeated it during television, radio, and print interviews, I hoped I wasn't going too far out on a limb. Today, I'm happy to report I haven't crashed to the ground.

My original hope was the timing would be right for *Second Acts* because this is a time of transition in which old rules have lost their power and new ones have yet to take hold. In other words, this is a unique time to order our own worlds and take charge of our own lives. What has made me even more confident that this is perfect time for a Second Act is the job market.

As I've traveled around talking to people across America about *Second Acts,* I've been struck by the response from those who are currently unemployed. Initially I was a bit hesitant to preach the *Second Acts* approach to people without work. After all, one of the largest and most common obstacles is lack of sufficient money. Someone who is without work, I initially thought, would be less open to the kind of leap of faith sometimes required to launch a Second Act. I couldn't have been more wrong.

The job market of 2003 is perhaps the worst we've seen in decades. We seem to be in the midst of a jobless economic recovery. Being forced to lower expectations, and still having to wait months or even a year to find new work, is now quite common. The current unemployment crisis may, God willing, actually be a short-term situation. But it seems to represent the onset of a long term under employment crisis. It seems clear most of those who lose their current jobs will find themselves working for less money in the future. It's a major accomplishment today if you can just maintain your income.

It's thrilling to see how many people, faced with this situation, are choosing to pursue a Second Act, to go after the life of their dreams. As one unemployed executive I met at a speaking engagement in Chicago said to me: "If I can't get a job making the kind of money I was before, why not just go after my dream instead? In some ways it's actually less of a financial sacrifice now than it would have been if I was still working." That's a sentiment I've heard over and over again in the past year. I've been inspired by the willingness of so many people to look at their current unemployment and their potential future under employment as opportunities to reinvent their lives.

Jenny Nosenko[1] is one person whose story I found particularly inspiring. Last year, Jenny was a successful business consultant employed by the consulting arm of a large well known financial services firm. After an accounting scandal sent her firm's fortunes into a tailspin, Jenny was one of hundreds of employees who found themselves out of work. She was able to negotiate a year's severance pay. Her husband Joshua, a high school math teacher, gave her a copy of *Second Acts* and encouraged her to think twice before she blindly jumped back into the job market. Josh said her severance and his salary would enable them and their two daughters—ten and eight years old—to get by with only a few sacrifices. Jenny went through the exercises in this book and decided she wanted to pursue a lifelong dream of writing a romance novel. Nine months later (Jenny calls the book her third child) she had a manuscript in hand. Using the marketing skills she previously preached to corporate clients, Jenny was able to land an agent who subsequently sold the book to a major publishing house. While the advance is less than ten percent of what she was previously earning, Jenny is ecstatic. She feels she's finally on the right path.

For almost a year now, I've been getting calls, emails, and letters from people like Jenny; people from all over America, of all ages, and in varied life circumstances, who have adopted the *Second Acts* approach and are in the process of remaking their lives. Bill Mushkin has started playing the piano again after years of ignoring it. Bill is playing piano one night a week in the lobby of a local hotel, while still keeping his full-time job as a sporting goods store manager, but he's happier than he has been in years. Paula Epstein, with the active support of her husband and teenage children, has decided to go back to college at night to pursue a degree in arts education, with the idea of becoming an art teacher.

Almost universally the people who contact me to talk about their Second Acts say it was the best decision they ever made. There truly is no better time to reinvent your life than right now. And to start all you need to do is turn the page.

—Stephen M. Pollan
August 2003

---

[1] The names and some of the details of the stories in this introduction have been changed to protect the individuals' privacy.

PART I

SETTING THE STAGE FOR YOUR SECOND ACT

"Often people attempt to live their lives backwards: they try to have more things, or more money, in order to do more of what they really want so that they will be happier. The way it actually works is the reverse. You must first be who you really are, then, do what you need to do, in order to have what you want."

—MARGARET YOUNG

CHAPTER 1

You Can Lead the Life of Your Dreams

"There are no second acts in American lives."

—F. SCOTT FITZGERALD

Fitzgerald was wrong. You can have a Second Act. You can lead the life you've always wished no matter your age or stage in life.

The dream you think has become impossible with advancing age, new obligations, or increased responsibility can be made real. The hope you've been deferring until a time when the stars are in perfect alignment can be fulfilled today. The goal you think out of reach because you've traveled an alternate path is still within your grasp.

You can give up your job as a stockbroker and pursue your youthful dream of becoming a professional photographer.

You can jump off the fast track and have a child, even though you're not married and have no intention of marrying.

You can pack up your family and move from the suburbs to the country, giving up your harried lifestyle for a more idyllic one.

You can leave a deadening retirement behind and go back to college to study art history.

You can give up having a business career and instead stay home to care for your children.

You can launch a business now, despite not having paid the dues the pundits demand.

You have an opportunity, not just to reinvent yourself, but to become your true self; to give expression to your suppressed hopes and dreams; to take the seed you've kept dormant in the dark within you, expose it to warmth and light, and let it burst forth into life.

Almost all of us have buried personal hopes and dreams. In order to please our parents, our friends, our spouses, our teachers, and our employers, we've molded our lives into what we think the outside world wants us to be.

To win and keep our parents' love, we've acted in certain ways and followed certain paths. We've become lawyers because they wanted us to be professionals. We married and had children because they wanted us to give them grandchildren. We lived a certain lifestyle, or lived in a certain place, because we knew it would gain their approval.

To become accepted, first by our friends, and then society at large, we have adopted certain attitudes and behaviors. Children work hard to fit into their peer group, adopting informal uniforms and language and habits that mark them as part of the pack. We never really left that desire to fit in behind as we grew older. We measured ourselves against our friends and peers. A teenager in the suburbs needs a car. A single twenty-something male in the city needs a thin girlfriend. A married thirty-something woman needs a baby. A senior needs successful grandchildren.

We've allowed the outside world to draw up schedules and checklists for us against which we judge our own worth. Haven't gotten married by thirty-five? Hopeless. Not earning $100,000 by forty? Loser. Haven't retired early and moved to the sunbelt? Failure.

Comparing ourselves to these external standards often brings misery and self hatred: Either we despise ourselves for not measuring up, or we despise ourselves for not being true to our own selves.

Good news. There's never been a better time to revolt against external standards and to be true to yourself. We're living in a transitionary time. Society, culture, and the economy are all shifting from the values of the past to new values, not yet fully formed. In this interregnum the old rules have lost most of their power, and new, potentially oppressive external standards haven't yet taken hold. As British Prime Minister Tony Blair has said of our time: "This is a moment to seize. The kaleidoscope has been shaken. The pieces are all in flux. Soon they will settle again. Before they do so, let us reorder this world around us." An opportunity like this doesn't come along in every lifetime. It comes, at most, once a century. We're lucky enough to be alive at this moment when anything is possible, at the moment perfect for Second Acts.

We're also lucky enough to be living in the United States of America. At the risk of sounding jingoistic, America is the land of Second Acts. Throughout our history people have come to these shores for just that purpose. Whether they were fleeing persecution, famine, war, genocide, oppression, or poverty, people from every corner of the world have come to America to reinvent themselves. The streets may not be paved with gold, but this is the land of milk and honey and opportunity. In America, you are not limited by your race, religion, color, gender, size, strength, appearance, language, or sexual orientation. Your only limits are self imposed.

You can have a Second Act. It doesn't matter if you're widowed, seventy years old and living on a fixed income. It doesn't matter if you've two kids in college and thousands of dollars in credit card debt. It doesn't matter if you're a workaholic professional, or a unemployed manager, or a burned out stockbroker, or a harried stay-at-home mom. I have helped all these people launch Second Acts. I can help you too.

GRANDMA MOSES

Anna Mary Robertson had a difficult life. Born in 1860 in upstate New York, she was sent out as a "hired girl" to work as a domestic on a neighboring farm. After 15 years as a servant, she married a "hired man," Thomas Salmon Moses, and together they moved to Virginia. For two decades they tried to make a go of it. Anna bore ten children, five of whom died in infancy. In 1905 she, her husband, and her five children moved back to upstate New York, settling in Eagle Bridge. In 1927 Thomas died. Always skilled at sewing and embroidery, Anna's work was admired by family and friends. At the age of 76 arthritis

Looking to live out a creative dream? We've been socialized to believe creative endeavors must come from the young and struggling. Youthful artistic success gains far more attention than mature work. The dark and dingy loft is thought to be the only place from which inspiration can spring. Yet for every Rimbaud bursting onto and off the scene like a comet, there's a Wallace Stevens. For every Basquiat, there's a Grandma Moses. And, for every Kerouac typing wildly in a railroad flat, there's a Pynchon living comfortably in suburbia. The notion that the youth culture is the only artistic culture is nonsense. Inspiration can be drawn from every stage in life and from every economic circumstance.

Does your dream involve motherhood? The typical age of marriage and maternity has fluctuated throughout American history. Assuming you're a baby boomer, your mother's generation may have gotten married in their late teens and given birth in the early

made it difficult for her to use a needle and thread. Her sister suggested she take up painting instead. Anna launched her Second Act. Her first works were exhibited at local fairs. An amateur art collector, seeing a collection of her works at a drug store, bought them all and then managed to have one included in a 1939 show of contemporary folk painting at New York's Museum of Modern Art. A dealer who saw the painting agreed to give her a one-woman show at his gallery. It was called "What a Farmwife Painted" and became a hit. A news report on the show used her home town nickname: Grandma Moses. By the 1950s she and her work were American icons. She died in 1961 at the age of 101, but her Second Act continues. Today she is revered as the original personification of "outsider art." ■

twenties, but your grandmother's generation delayed both marriage and maternity due to economic and political factors. Thanks to advances in medical science, it's no longer unusual for a 40 year old to have a child. If insurmountable physical or biological difficulties exist, adoption is accepted more than ever before. And wider acceptance also extends to both natural and adoptive single motherhood as well. Are there still hurdles to conquer? Certainly. Will it require effort and persistence? Of course. But becoming a mother is both possible and practical.

Is your dream to plant roots early in rural splendor, rather than start life in a studio apartment? Again, assuming you're a boomer, the real-estate patterns of your parents' generation aren't rules you must follow religiously. You don't need to move from urban starter apartment in your mid-twenties, to suburban family home in your mid-thirties, to sunbelt retirement condo in your mid-sixties.

Information technology and transportation are so advanced that an exurban or rural home could work for you at any stage in life, in any profession or business. Telecommuting and flex-time options are more common. Travel can become productive work time. Will it require compromise? Clearly. Are there issues you'd need to iron out? Obviously. But there's no reason you can't live where and how you dream.

Is entrepreneurship part of your dream? While there have been demographic trends throughout the history of American entrepreneurship, technology and improved health now make it possible for anyone of any age to start a business. Society's attitudes toward both older and younger workers have changed, partly by design and partly by default. Not only are older individuals more active today than in the past, with work involving less physical strength and stamina than ever before, but there's a greater societal need for older workers and entrepreneurs. Younger individuals with only a marketing or technological vision and no other business experience have started some of the most successful ventures of the past decade. An entrepreneurial failure at age twenty-two or fifty-two won't stand in the way of future employment opportunities. In many ways it could help. The personal arguments against starting a business are also specious. Could starting a business later in life put your retirement savings and child education savings at risk? Perhaps. If you're only twenty-two might you find it tough to get financial backing? Of course. But entrepreneurial challenges are essentially the same regardless of your age.

No one has a right to tell you, "No, you can't do that," or "You must do this"—not even that negative and domineering voice in your head. There's no scorecard or measuring stick you need compare yourself against other than the one in your own heart. Ultimately, there's nothing that stands in your way other than internal inhibitions, insecurities, and fears.

Your Second Act won't be painless. You may need to make sacrifices and compromises. You might need to learn new skills and jargon. And, it may take some time. But a new life of substance and meaning can't be built in a day. This is one instance when a little pain and a bit of fear are probably good things. If your Second Act is painless and you're not afraid of it, you're not launching the new life you truly desire.

I know you have it in your power to do whatever you want. My name is Stephen M. Pollan. I'm an attorney and life coach in New York City. In the more than twenty-five years I've been in private practice, I've helped hundreds of people launch Second Acts. I've helped people make dramatic transitions: from stockbroker to photographer; from career woman to single mother; from urbanite to country dweller; from retiree to college student; from plumber to restauranteur; from college student to entrepreneur; and from actor to activist.

All these individuals doubted they could launch a Second Act, just as you probably doubt you can. But they all knew there was something missing in their lives; that in some way—large or small, personal or professional—they weren't leading the lives of their dreams. They felt they had reached a dead end.

"WHAT AM I WAITING FOR?"

Arthur and Donna McCarty[1] thought their golden years were preordained. Chief financial officer of a multinational telecommunications company, sixty-two-year-old Arthur had been making an

---

[1] Throughout this book, I'll be using real people as examples. They're almost all clients of mine. As such, I'm obliged to protect their privacy. That's why I've changed their names and altered enough details of their lives to make their identities less obvious. Rest assured, none of the salient points have been altered.

exceptional salary for more than two decades. A short, stocky man with closely cropped, curly gray hair, he radiates power. Donna, his wife of thirty years, is a tall, thin brunette, ten years his junior. A senior editor at a major publishing house, her Town & Country image belied a working-class upbringing. With both their sons happily married and ensconced in homes and careers, Arthur and Donna had sold their suburban Westchester County home and were splitting time between a lovely Upper East Side apartment and a weekend home in Northwestern Connecticut. Retirement was a long-term, still indistinct goal. . . something to think about when they were older.

Then the telecommunications industry collapsed. The value of shares in Arthur's firm plummeted. While his stock options took a hit, Arthur had diversified and wasn't too worried. He knew the industry would bounce back in another five to seven years, just about the time he thought he'd retire. But his company's low share price attracted attention and soon the firm was purchased by a larger, European-based competitor. Arthur, a valued executive for more than forty years, was, to use the new chairman's term, "redundant." He was offered an early retirement package with the not-so-subtle message that if he didn't accept it, he'd receive a far less generous termination package. A long-time client of mine—I had helped him and Donna sell their suburban home and buy their apartment and weekend place a decade earlier—he came to me for help in maximizing the golden parachute. Unhappy at the prospect of being retired at sixty-two, Arthur began exploring his options.

Four months later, Arthur and Donna were sitting in my office. They told me Donna's career was soaring. Publishing wasn't immune to recessions, but Donna's track record of acquiring and publishing bestsellers ensured she'd weather any downsizing. "That's great," I said. "What can I help you with today?" I asked. Arthur looked at Donna, who averted her eyes for a moment and then began telling me a story. "We were having breakfast one morning when Arthur told me he was meeting with a headhunter to explore opportunities with not-for-profit agencies and philanthropic organizations," she began. "I immediately thought that would be a perfect fit since, like me, Arthur was brought up in a home steeped in the ethos of social activism. During my cab ride to the office, I was thinking about how Arthur and I had always assumed that when I hit sixty and he reached seventy we'd retire to Florida, do some volunteer work, and take trips. My telephone was ringing when I stepped into the office. I picked it up. It was one of the other editors telling me about an emergency trip I needed to schedule. Apparently our company was competing for a tell-all book by the estranged spouse of some philandering Congressman who'd been all over the news. I was tapped to fly down to D.C. to meet with her. I hung up the telephone and was overwhelmed by the disparity between where I was and where I wanted to be. It was tough to resist the urge to quit right there and then." "Why did you resist the urge?" I asked.

"I HAVE NOTHING THAT REALLY MATTERS."

Dani Kaplan was living the life she'd always dreamed. At thirty-nine, she was editorial director of a family of six glossy entertainment magazines, published by a division of a media company with holdings in the film, Internet, publishing, radio, and television industries. A petite, raven-haired, single woman whose tastes ran to Mercedes, Manolo Blahniks, and mink, she had become a fixture in the hybrid social scene where fashion, publishing, and entertainment merged.

Dani had first come to me five years earlier for help in negotiating her employment contract. It was a complex deal, because she was living at that time in Beverly Hills and working for a film studio in Los Angeles. Although she loved the California weather and lifestyle and had finally bought the Mercedes 450 SLC of her fantasies, her heart was in New York. Born and raised in the Northern New Jersey suburbs of New York City, she longed to come back East. I helped her negotiate a lucrative and secure contract, which enabled her to afford a garage for the Mercedes she refused to give up, and then began to help her look for real estate. Dani knew it would make more sense to buy an apartment than rent, but for all her external confidence, she found the idea of a single woman carrying a mortgage troubling. However, after going over the numbers with her and sending her out to visit apartments, she came around. Dani felt that, at this point in her life, career and finances had to come first. There would be time for marriage and family in the future, after she'd reached all her job and money goals. She imagined that in a few years she'd meet an older, successful, professional man. They'd marry, buy an apartment by Central Park, have a child, and live happily ever after. But for now, work came first.

One morning in mid September 2001, I picked up my telephone and heard Dani's voice. I knew that, like me, she was usually at her desk by 8:30 a.m., regardless of how late she was out the night before. She knew she could get a great deal done before 10:00 a.m., when most of the publishing industry finally struggled into work, and she'd be able to get hold of most of the corporate types, who also tended to be at work early. She told me that two weeks earlier she'd been sitting at her desk, alone in the office, when she heard a loud whooshing sound, followed by a low rumble that shook the building's windows. Looking south out the window in the reception area she saw billowing smoke. Her administrative assistant and one of the junior editors arrived in time to see the second plane hit. "Instinctively, I told the junior editor to go down to the lobby and tell the security guard that the magazine was closing for the day and that any employees who arrived should be told to go home," Dani reported. "Then my assistant Fiona and I split up the list of employees and began telephoning each, telling them to stay home if they hadn't left, or leaving a message if they already had. With that done," she continued, "Fiona broke down crying. She had spoken to her husband who told her to go pick up their daughter and bring her home from school right away." Dani began to choke up. "I grabbed my cell phone and lap top, and the two of us left the office. I put Fiona in a cab and then walked home, alone, to my apartment. When I got there, I looked around and felt that I didn't have everything. . . I had nothing. Fiona had a husband and daughter. I had a cell phone and lap top."

"HOW COME I'M NOT DOING WHAT I WANT?"

Barry and Maria D'Angelo had always done exactly what they were supposed to do. They met while undergraduates at Cornell University, where Barry was majoring in restaurant administration and Maria was studying design. Barry looks like Andy Garcia. He's animated and outgoing, quick with a joke and a slap on the back. Maria is short and demure. She's too attractive to be called mousey, but she seems to naturally slip into the background, leaving center stage entirely to Barry. Both grew up in bedroom communities on the south shore of Long Island. Maria is the only child of two teachers. Barry's father ran a school bus leasing company while his mom stayed home and raised him. After graduating college, they returned to Long Island, married, and bought a starter home. Barry became assistant manager of a catering hall—he calls it a wedding factory—while Maria landed a job with a textile firm. In short order, she became pregnant, and

Barry started his own business: a pub-style restaurant, financed initially by his father. Maria was soon able to stay at home because Barry's restaurant thrived. In three years there was another child and another restaurant location. By the time I met them, Barry owned four restaurants, all of which were doing very well.

They first came to see me about seven years ago. Barry's father had died, leaving his widow a large estate and Barry the bus leasing business. Barry's restaurant business had become problematic. Although he loved the excitement, he admitted the long hours were putting stress on his marriage. The bus leasing business, while not very exciting, was a cash cow. We determined that Barry could almost double his annual income by selling the restaurants and investing the proceeds, while taking over management of his father's business. Besides, he'd be able to spend more time at home with his family. "What's to think about," he asked rhetorically, before giving his okay to the sale.

From then on I'd see the D'Angelos once or twice a year to deal with financial and legal issues that came up—the purchase of a new home, financing a child's college tuition, updating wills. Interestingly enough, over time Maria became more outgoing, but I realized that was because Barry had turned his personality down a notch or two. I thought perhaps he had matured and no longer needed the spotlight to himself.

I learned there was more to it when Barry came to my office in the summer of 2001. After exchanging the usual pleasantries and asking after each other's families, Barry told me that the previous week he had been to the funeral of his uncle. The younger brother of his father, Barry's uncle had been an art teacher in the New York City public schools for more than forty years. Upon retirement he moved to Utah to teach at a school on a Native American reservation. Barry's father had always bemoaned his brother's lack of financial success and criticized his downwardly mobile lifestyle. "At the funeral, one of my uncle's former students said something that cut me to the quick," Barry explained. "She said my uncle was an inspiration to his students because he spent his life doing what he loved." I tried to comfort Barry, offering some platitudes about family. "I'm not crying because of *his death*. I'm crying because of *my life*. I'm envious of him."

Almost every week I help people like these, rich and poor, young and old, famous and unknown, create the lives of their dreams and build the careers they've always wanted. I can help you reinvent yourself. I can help you launch a Second Act. My confidence comes, not just because I've helped others do it, but because I did it myself.

"GREAT NEWS: YOU HAVE TUBERCULOSIS."

In 1978, I was forty-eight years old. My wife, Corky, and I were living in a lovely apartment in Manhattan, having moved from suburban Long Island. I was under contract as a senior vice president at an international commercial bank. I reported directly to the chairman and was responsible for turning troubled real-estate investments into profitable assets. The bank had sought me out for the position because it had dealt with me when I ran an American Stock Exchange listed venture capital firm.

I was good at my job, and I loved it. If you looked up "workaholic" in the dictionary, you'd find my picture. I was at my desk down at 44 Wall Street by 7 a.m. I didn't get back to our apartment on the Upper East Side until 10 p.m. I was making an excellent living. I was also eating badly and smoking at least three packs of cigarettes a day. The only part of me getting any exercise was my elbow.

My wife wasn't working outside the home. In fact, she had gone back to college to get her Masters degree. My oldest child, my son Michael, was a student at Bennington College and had just come back from a semester at Oxford. My other three children, my daughters Lori, Tracy, and Dana, were all going to a private high school in Manhattan.

I was driven to succeed. I didn't really communicate with my wife and children. I had no hobbies and few friends. I was too busy climbing Mount Olympus.

I had been feeling under the weather for about a month before I finally decided to go see our family doctor. He heard my dry hacking cough, listened to my labored breathing, and decided to send me for a chest X-ray. Two days later he called and said there was a suspicious black spot on one of my lungs. He wanted me to be tested for tuberculosis and to take another X-ray. The tuberculosis test came back negative. The second X-ray showed the spot was still there. My doctor ordered a biopsy. Corky worried about my health. I worried about how much work I was missing.

One of my most vivid memories is of sitting up in my hospital bed after the biopsy procedure, with my wife standing at my side, while we watched and listened to three doctors arguing about my lung as if I wasn't even there. The biopsy results weren't clear, and my family doctor, who had a great deal of experience with tuberculosis, wanted to take a culture before he agreed with the other two doctors that I had lung cancer. I felt like I was just a bystander to my life, and perhaps death. Corky and I spent the next 24 hours thinking about, but not talking about, my death.

I was sitting at our kitchen table when the telephone rang early on a Wednesday morning. It was my doctor. He said, "Great news: you have tuberculosis."

I felt like I had been given my life back. It was if a 100-pound sand bag that was lying on my chest had been lifted. My wife and I cried and hugged. Then, as the joy and relief slowly eased, we started to examine our situation.

I worked for the bank on an annual contract basis. We had been in the midst of negotiating my renewal when I took the first X-ray. This wasn't a "family-style" organization. It wasn't as if I were a branch manager with roots in a community. I was a suit. The rest of the executives at the headquarters were as single-minded and driven as I. All I could expect from the bank was a lovely bouquet of flowers. That meant I had no job.

We had a big mortgage on our apartment. We had taken out loans to pay for private school for my daughters and college for my son. We had no savings. Thank God I had disability insurance, which I had been talked into buying eight years earlier.[2] The doctor told me I'd be on a heavy regimen of drugs and would be physically weak for quite some time. He didn't know how long treatment would last but assumed I would be out of work for about a year. Corky and I determined the disability payments would cover about 60 percent of our expenses.

I had incredibly mixed feelings. On the one hand, I was grateful to God for having spared my life. For the first time I truly felt gratitude to something outside myself. On the other hand, I was frightened. We had tremendous bills, no savings, and I had no job prospects. I suggested to Corky that we sell our home to bring in some money and lower our expenses. I could see her think about it for a moment. Then she turned to me and said, "No. I don't think we'll be able to replace it when you're better." Suddenly, I realized that she had hope. She was thinking about life after my illness. She believed in a better tomorrow. She believed I could launch a Second Act. She was right.

---

[2] To this day I am, outside of an agent, the world's strongest advocate for disability insurance. It saved me and my family. When a new client comes to see me I tell him or her to do two things if we're going to have an ongoing relationship. First, get a full medical exam. Second, buy more disability insurance than your company gives you.

Believe it or not, I now thank God every day for giving me tuberculosis. That's because I feel like I'm doing more than just personal consulting: I think I'm offering people their own renaissance, a chance to live two lives in one, a Second Act.

I believe that when you keep your dreams locked away in inner darkness, they begin to eat away at your soul. But, by exposing those repressed dreams to the light and pursuing them, you lift your soul to unimagined heights. Simply by raising the curtain on your Second Act, giving yourself the possibility of a new life, you begin to feel like a new person. Reinvent yourself, and you'll experience more added joy and contentment than you can imagine. A Second Act doesn't just change the specific aspect of your life that you're reinventing; it invigorates your entire life.

LAUNCH A SECOND ACT AND FEEL OPTIMISTIC ABOUT THE FUTURE.

That happened to Adrienne Laval, sixty-three, and her husband Frank, sixty-seven. The Lavals retired early to Florida in order to be able to play golf and tennis year round. When Frank turned sixty-two, he and Adrienne calculated they'd be able to live well on Frank's pension, Social Security, and the proceeds from the sale of their home in Cleveland Heights. Their first four years in Florida were all they'd hoped. But then Frank started feeling out of sorts. He was having a harder time playing eighteen holes. One of his regular foursome broke a hip and had to give up golf. One of the guys he played poker with had a stroke. For the first time in his life, Frank started to feel, and worse yet, act his age. He began obsessing over his death, dwelling on his legacy, and worrying excessively about what would happen to Adrienne if he died suddenly. "It was as if he was just waiting to die," Adrienne told me on a visit two years ago. "He'd stopped looking forward to the future."

Today, the Lavals are owners of a ice cream and frozen yogurt stand in South Florida. Their Second Act may not have given Frank the energy to play thirty-six holes a day, but he has stopped obsessing about his mortality and is instead planning on opening a second location and perhaps offering sandwiches as well.

LAUNCH A SECOND ACT AND ENJOY EACH MOMENT OF LIFE.

That's what Mitchell Lewis discovered. A forty-three-year-old free-lance graphic artist, living and working from a farmhouse three hours north of New York, Mitchell and his wife, Debra, consciously chose not to have children so they would be able to live a certain lifestyle. Both are self employed. They travel and entertain frequently. Mitchell and Debra eschewed debt in order to retain the freedom to shift directions if they chose. But despite all this, Mitchell found himself obsessively focusing on the things he hadn't accomplished, both personally and professionally. "I'm feeling that time is running out," he told me eighteen months ago. "At first I started prioritizing my time but then, rather than focusing on what I was doing, I started thinking about what I might never be able to do."

Today, Mitchell is painting watercolor landscapes as he dreamed back as college. His Second Act involves taking booths on the small town art show circuit and showing his work in a handful of upstate New York galleries. "I'm making less money in a month then I used to in a week," he admits, "but I'm loving my life and fully living every single moment of it."

LAUNCH A SECOND ACT AND EXPERIENCE A CREATIVE BURST.

Barbara Mitchell, fifty-seven, needed just that kind of burst. The child of two educators, she was raised to be a school teacher. For more than thirty years she had been teaching English to middle-school students. Whenever others joked about how dealing with a pack of twelve- and thirteen-year-olds must be a nightmare, she'd laugh and disagree, explaining that their energy fed her creativity. But, on a recent visit she told me she'd found it harder to rouse the creative impulse. This school year, she admitted, she didn't bother developing a new course outline or updating her notes or bulletin boards. She felt she just couldn't come up with any new ideas.

Barbara launched a Second Act and experienced renewed creativity and self expression. Interestingly, in her Second Act she's still a middle-school English teacher. Going through the process brought her full circle. Over the years, the bureaucracy and the politics of her district and department had become the focus of Barbara's mental energies. Barbara's Second Act enabled her to set all those distractions aside and once again focus on her true calling: teaching children. Barbara has rediscovered some essential core element of her personality or psyche she felt had been lost.

LAUNCH A SECOND ACT
AND FEEL CLOSER TO GOD.

Cary McConnell's Second Act has brought her closer to God. The twenty-nine-year-old single woman had become a nurse to ease peoples' suffering and pain. An average student in high school, Cary had dedicated herself to her studies and progressed from a community college, to nursing school, to a job at New York's Sloan Kettering Hospital. For five years she dealt with death and dying on an almost daily basis. Cary told me she had seen "good deaths" and "bad deaths;" she had seen some people accept their fate, and others fight to the very end. A devout Christian, Cary said the hospital was an uplifting place for the first three years she worked there. But by the time she came to see me, the lack of justice she perceived in the world had made her very angry with

God. She had a hard time finding meaning in her work. She confessed her prayers were offering little solace.

Three years later, having launched a Second Act, Cary's work and prayers are far more fulfilling. She feels closer to God than ever. Cary went back to school and is now a nurse practitioner, working at a large obstetrics and gynecological practice in western Long Island.

LAUNCH A SECOND ACT AND FEEL CLOSER TO OTHERS.

Tim Kaplan was able to reconnect with his partner, Ben Linden, after launching his Second Act. Ben and Tim had been together for almost fifteen years when they first came to see me. Ben, forty, is a successful financial planner, very driven to advance in his career. Tim, forty-four, was working as a dental hygienist. Unlike Ben, Tim had always worked to live, rather than lived to work. They had always shared chores and responsibilities, but in the past year Tim has been apathetic at best, distant at worst. Ben told me he kept asking Tim if there was something wrong. "Tim's response was invariably a variation of 'I'm just having a bad day,'" Ben explained. "The bad days have now stretched into a bad year," Tim admitted. "I need a change," he stressed.

Finally deciding he should try to work at something he loved, Tim went to school to become a dog groomer. As he joked to me just recently, "I may be constantly covered in pet hair, but at least I'm communicating."

LAUNCH A SECOND ACT AND DEVELOP PATIENCE.

Reinventing himself actually kept Dennis Kent from acting rashly. The thirty-four-year-old Brooklynite is a third-generation lawyer

Famous Second Act

TOM CLANCY

In 1984, lifelong military technology buff Tom Clancy was a thirty-seven-year-old insurance broker looking to launch a Second Act. His first novel, *The Hunt for Red October*, a realistic tale of the defection of a Russian nuclear submarine, was published by a small publishing house specializing in naval history. Thanks to its crafting and accuracy, it became a favorite of the military and eventually ended up on the reading list of President Ronald Reagan, who praised it publicly. It was soon a bestseller. Since then, ten of Clancy's books have been number one on *The New York Times* bestseller list. More than fifty million copies of his books have been printed. Three have been made into major motion pictures, and a fourth film adaptation is on the way. ■

who graduated from the same law school and joined the same firm as his father and grandfather. He and his wife, Maria, the daughter of first-generation Cuban immigrants, created a warm home life for their daughters, five and three. Two years ago, Dennis and Maria came to my office for a visit. Dennis revealed he had become moody and was bringing his work home emotionally. "I was so pleased when two nights ago he came home with the old bounce in his step," Maria told me. "Yeah," Dennis interrupted, "but your joy vanished when I told you I wanted to quit the firm the next day and go to cooking school." Dennis told me he felt this was his sole remaining shot at doing what he wanted in life.

By setting aside his rashness and by going through all the exercises outlined in this book, Dennis was able to launch his Second Act as a reasoned, well thought-out process, rather than as single spontaneous act. Dennis was both able to reinvent himself and rediscover patience. He was also able to keep his wife from losing her mind. Today, he owns and manages a successful Caribbean-style restaurant in Greenwich Village.

Skeptical that I can really help you live the life of your dreams? Maybe you think you're too old or too young. Perhaps you feel your opportunity has passed. Certain that you can't afford it? Or, are you doubtful launching a Second Act can really improve your life in all the ways I've outlined. Don't worry: I'm not insulted by your disbelief. Almost everyone is initially dubious when I say you can launch a Second Act, and it will turn your life from black and white to technicolor.

All I'm asking is you give me a chance to outline my program. What do you have to lose? Having picked up this book, I think I'm safe in assuming either you feel somewhat uneasy, dissatisfied, or unhappy with your current life, or you've a buried dream you'd like to resurrect and pursue. You're fed up with being fed up. Give me the opportunity to show you how I reinvented myself, and how I help other people, like you, reinvent their lives.

To raise the curtain on your Second Act all you need do is give voice to your dream.

CHAPTER 2

Putting Your
Dream into Words

"Dreams come true; without that possibility, nature would not incite us to have them."

—JOHN UPDIKE

What is your dream?

For some that's an easy question to answer. Maybe you've spent years, even decades, nurturing deep within you the spark of an idea for a business or a new career. Or, perhaps you've always had a fully developed fantasy vision of what you wished your life could be. Late at night when you can't sleep you draw solace from your dream. At times when your real world is frustrating or demoralizing, you look inward to your dream for the strength to go on. "One day I'll give this all up and write that novel I've been thinking about since college," you may think. Or, maybe you bite your tongue and swallow anger at your boss, or a client, thinking, "Just a few more years of this, and I'll have enough money to quit and open that bed and breakfast in Vermont."

Others don't have a fully developed dream. Instead of having completely drawn mental schematics of your fantasy life, you may have an abstract sense of what you want. Maybe it's less a matter of what you want than what you don't want. On a crowded commuter train heading home late one night you think to yourself, "I need to figure out a way to work from home so the kids don't grow up without me." Or perhaps, sitting on a New England beach one morning while on vacation, with the gulls crying and a sea breeze blowing you say to yourself, "One day we'll leave the city and live by the ocean."

THE PROCESS IS IMPORTANT

Whether you've a full blueprint of your dream or just a vague notion, to launch the Second Act that will make it a reality, you need to define it clearly and simply. I think the best way to do that is to reduce it to its essential elements. It's a process I call *dream distillation*.

First, a note of warning to those who've spent a lifetime nurturing a specific dream. Please don't let your long-term devotion to your ideal life lead you to skip this process or give it only a few minutes of attention. I don't believe there's one grand, immutable design for your life, assigned by God or fate or circumstance at the moment of your birth. While it's possible to truly have the same dream your entire life, it's also possible your dream has changed. Just because you've notebooks and diaries filled with years of to-do lists for launching the little gift shop you dreamed of back in college, doesn't mean that's really your dream today. Our dreams and hopes can change as we grow and change and learn. Although there's nothing wrong with having the same passion at fifty as at twenty, there's also nothing wrong with acknowledging your passions have changed.

Sometimes, particularly as you come to terms with your mortality, the "roads not taken" become paved with gold in your imagination. As you accept that your time on Earth is finite, it's not uncommon to project all the things you may have missed out on, all the opportunities you sense have slipped away, onto a path you didn't follow: "If I had only become a lawyer I'd have been able to travel, buy a beach house, and send my kids to Ivy League colleges." Although that may be true, it could also be that you've projected your hopes on a dream that's not worthy of them. It would be a shame for you to spend time and effort on a dream that's really just an outdated emotional reaction to your past rather than your current true calling.

Similarly, any unhappiness you may feel at your current circumstances could make a long-held fantasy seem all the more alluring. It's like a psychological version of the "grass is always greener" phenomenon. Your dream life magically has all the things lacking in your day-to-day life, and, incredibly, has none of the difficulties you face in your real world: "If we'd have moved to the country rather than stayed in the city, my marriage would be better, and the kids wouldn't be getting into trouble." Perhaps, but it's just as likely your life would lack the same or similar things, and you'd face equal or parallel obstacles. It would be terrible to dedicate yourself to a path that's a reaction to your current circumstances rather than a deeply held desire.

It would be equally terrible to automatically discount the path you're already on. Because you're reading this book, it's obvious you're not ecstatic about every aspect of your life. You're looking for a Second Act, so that means there's something lacking in your first act, the life you're currently leading. Who am I to disagree with you? However, I'd like to ask a favor. Keep an open mind while you're going through the exercises in this chapter. It just might be that you're already on the path of your dreams, but it's so overgrown with weeds and brush that you can't see it clearly. There are times when, like Dorothy in *The Wizard of Oz*, it takes a journey of self discovery to realize "there's no place like home."

In the previous chapter, I introduced you to Barbara Mitchell, the 57-year-old middle-school English teacher who launched a

---

ROSEANNE BARR

After a confused and troubled childhood in Salt Lake City, Utah, punctuated by an eight-month stay in a mental institution, seventeen-year-old Roseanne Barr left home on a bus and settled in Georgetown, Colorado. There, she met and married Bill Pentland, a motel night clerk. She and her husband had three children. Living in a trailer and working as a cocktail waitress, Barr began humorously cutting down men who made passes at her. Customers loved her "act" and encouraged her to pursue comedy. Her Second Act began. Working in punk rock clubs and motorcycle bars, she developed a razor sharp, uniquely female style. In 1985 she was hired to work at the Comedy Store in Los Angeles, and the family moved west. A string of successful television appearances was soon followed by the offer to star in a sitcom centering on the everyday problems of a working-class family. The show was a huge success, running for nine years and making the former cocktail waitress a very wealthy woman. ■

Second Act while maintaining all the outer trappings of her life. By going through the process in this and subsequent chapters, she rediscovered the things she loved about her work and her life. Hers wasn't a unique case. Although a minority, such Second Acts aren't uncommon. For example, Debra Mushkin, a thirty-four-year-old freelance writer, came to me five years ago looking for a Second Act. Like Barbara, after going through the process Debra rediscovered everything she loved about writing. Her writing is still going strong: She recently sold two romance novels and is at work on a third.

FIVE EXERCISES TO HELP YOU DEFINE YOUR DREAM

With all those cautions in place, let's start distilling and defining your dream. The idea here is go through five exercises that reveal what it is you want to do with your life and then enable you to frame it in as specific a manner as possible. The first three exercises look at your dream or dreams from slightly different perspectives in an effort to give you a number of different views of the issue. By analyzing your passions, your strengths and weaknesses, and your interests, you may be able to get a fix on what it is you truly want. The remaining two exercises help frame your dream in as accurate and specific a way as possible. By first looking to see whether your dream is really an underlying need, and then by refining your dream, we'll make it that much easier to achieve.

There's no requirement for you to go through each of these exercises. However, I've found that the more of these you put yourself through, the more insights you gain, and that the more insights you gain, the quicker you'll be able to achieve your dream. The choice is yours: Spend a few more days now doing the tough self analysis or spend a few more years later.

There's also no requirement for you to put your responses in writing. But again, I'd urge you to do so. I've learned that recording your thoughts and conclusions on paper is incredibly valuable, not just in launching Second Acts, but in tackling almost any obstacle. I believe in physically writing up plans for everything from conversations with your parents to starting a new business.

In fact, Chapter 13 will center on the creation of a formal written script for your Second Act. Until then, let me just note that putting your thoughts in writing will not only provide you with a therapeutic tool, but it will also give you a roadmap you can follow throughout the process. Months from now, when you're frustrated over some particular task, you'll be able to turn to your script and see the reason why it's important. Or, if a day comes when you just want to give up, when you can't quite remember why you're trying to overcome a particular obstacle, you'll be able to turn to your script and see, in black and white, why you're making the effort.

The specific form of your notes is up to you. For now, just find yourself a new notebook or pad. Or, if you'd prefer, open a new folder on your laptop or PDA. I'll be referring to this record of your thoughts, actions, and progress as your Second Act notebook.

Exercise 1

Turn to a blank page in your new notebook and title it PASSIONS. What are the things you feel passionately about? Write them down. Don't worry about their practicality or their potential for generating income. We're not building the whole house right now, just pouring a foundation. Don't start defending yourself to your critics or planning ways to defeat obstacles. Give free rein to your feelings. Love to paint watercolor landscapes? Write it down. Enjoy shopping for old toys at yard sales? Make a note of it. Get a thrill from writing the jokey newsletter for the company softball team? Put it on the list.

Next, come up with lists of places, not things, you feel passionate about. Don't limit yourself to places you've lived or even visited. It's fine to include the lake you summer at every year, but it's also okay to include the ruins of Ancient Troy if you've always

Famous Second Act

JACK KEMP

In retrospect, Jack French Kemp seems to have been working on his Second Act while still in the middle of his first. A graduate of Occidental College in California, Kemp was starting quarterback and captain of the football team. After doing post graduate work in political science and education and serving on active duty in the Army Reserves, he was drafted by the San Diego Chargers of the American Football League. Traded to Buffalo in 1963, Kemp led the Bills to two consecutive league championships in 1964 and 1965. He also

wanted to go there. And, don't feel they need to be specific geographic places either. Do you just love browsing through piles of old dusty volumes at used book stores? Write it down. Love the palpable sense of energy and excitement at a theater when the curtain is about to go up? List it.

Finally, think back to the times you felt the best about yourself. Don't focus on just milestone events—such as the birth of a child—or the usual suspects—like your wedding day. Really dig down for those special days that stand out in your mind. What were you doing? Where were you? Who were your with? It could be the morning you went for a bicycle ride with your husband over the rolling dunes of Martha's Vineyard. Or, it could be an afternoon when you were sitting on your deck with your child in your lap waiting for the burgers on the grill to be done. In retrospect, what was it about those instances that made them singular? Write it all down.

cofounded the AFL Players Association and served as its president five times. Always interested in politics and active in community service projects, Kemp decided to retire from football and launch his Second Act by running for Congress in 1971. He served Buffalo for nine terms as a Congressman, making a name for himself by combining conservative supply side economic ideas with a passion for racial justice and urban revitalization. He served as Secretary for Housing and Urban Development in the first Bush administration and was later tapped as Bob Dole's vice presidential running mate in 1996. After that defeat, Kemp began working with Empower America and Habitat for Humanity. ■

Take a few days to look back at all you've written. Read your lists over and over. Look for links that join items together. See whether you can find threads that run through the lists. Let all the good feelings the lists evoke wash over you. Don't belittle any of your passions, disparage any of the locations you've listed, or discount the importance of an otherwise minor event you've singled out. This list is for you and you alone. There's no one whose feelings you need to protect or whom you need to impress. To come up with your true dream, you need to be self-centered, but in a good way. Focus on yourself alone.

With some reflection now under your belt, I want you to engage in a little fantasizing. Turn to a fresh page and label it WINDFALL. You've just won the Powerball Lottery. We're not talking $3 million, pretaxes, shared with all your thirty-seven coworkers. We're talking $30 million, after taxes, and it's all yours. What are you going to do with the money? Go ahead, list all the things you'd buy: high-definition home theater system, house in the South of France, matching Jaguars for you and your spouse; breast enlargement surgery or liposuction. Give full voice to your materialism. Then, note all the good things you'd do with money: open a no-kill animal shelter, endow a scholarship fund at your alma mater, buy your mother a new house. Express all your altruistic tendencies.

Have you had fun? Well, you've still got tens of millions of dollars left over. You've bought everything you've ever wanted and done everything you've ever wanted to do for others. Be a little selfish and give some thought to what you want to do for yourself. All this fantasy money gives you the chance to buy the life you've always wanted to lead. Maybe there's a location where you've always wanted to live. Perhaps there's someone you'd like to share this fantasy life with. Let go of your inhibitions and enjoy daydreaming. Think about it overnight.

When you wake up the next morning open your notebook to another fresh page or open another new document. Answer these two questions:

- What do I want?
- How will I know when I get it?

Dani Names Her Passions

By the time Dani Kaplan was ready to answer those questions she had made some surprising discoveries about her dream. If you recall, Dani is the thirty-nine-year-old, single woman from New York City who came to me saying that despite her outwardly successful, materially comfortable world, she felt her life was meaningless. After a couple of sessions I sent Dani home with the same homework assignment I just outlined for you.

Dani began by listing her passions. She loved shopping for silver jewelry and designer clothing. She could spend hours looking for just the right toys for her nieces and nephews. Even though she was New York City born and bred, she loved taking long summer drives along the coast with the top of her car down. Dani loved to cook and entertain at her apartment.

Next, Dani noted the places she adored. First was the flea market on 24th Street in Manhattan. Then there was the Pacific Coast Highway just north of San Francisco. Worth Avenue in Palm Beach made the list, as did FAO Schwartz during November and December. She'd always wanted to stroll the Ponte Vecchio in Florence and have a picnic at the Luxembourg Gardens in Paris.

Dani then turned to the times she felt best about herself. One was when she was able to present her parents with a new car she had bought for them after getting her first big bonus. Then there was the time she was a huge hit by making a speech at a television awards show. One of her favorite times was when she and her ten-year-old niece, Aimie, spent the day together at the Bronx Zoo, taking in all the sites, smells, tastes, and sounds. Finally, there was the afternoon she and an old boyfriend walked hand in hand for hours along a beach in Cape Cod, without seeing another soul or saying a word.

After thinking about her lists for a few days, Dani then worked on her lottery exercise. She wrote that she'd buy herself a new Mercedes, a summer house in the Hamptons, and a townhouse on Gramercy Park. She'd buy her parents a home in Florida and hire a nurse to care for her ailing father so her mother could have more of a life. She'd set aside money so her nieces and nephews could go to Ivy League universities. She'd give her older sister enough money so she could get out of her unhappy marriage and start fresh. And, with the money left? Dani thought about it overnight.

The next morning, over coffee at the diner around the corner from her apartment, Dani wrote in her diary that she'd find a wonderful husband, have a child, hire a full-time housekeeper/ nanny to help them, and they'd spend their lives and money traveling the world, spoiling their child. What did she want? To have a family life. How would she know when she got it? When she couldn't wait to get home from the office.

Exercise 2

Head a fresh page in your notebook STRENGTHS & WEAK-NESSES. What are you good at? Don't just note your skills. Make sure to mention your best physical, emotional, and psychological traits. No one is perfect, so list your failings as well. Certainly write down skills you lack, but also make note of any physical, emotional, or psychological flaws you've noticed in yourself. I know these are hard questions to answer objectively. That's for a couple of reasons.

Your ego can get in the way of the truth. You may, for whatever reason, be incredibly self critical, refusing to give yourself credit for anything, believing you're ugly, stupid, and inept. On the other hand, you might be a bit pompous and think that anything that has gone wrong in the past was someone else's fault or the failing of something outside yourself.

Questions about your strengths and weaknesses have also become clichés. I'm sure you're familiar with job interviewers who ask these questions, and you're equally familiar with all the superficially honest answers, which are actually efforts at spinning yourself into a job offer. ("I guess one of my flaws is that I'm an obsessive workaholic . . . I just won't quit until the last *i* is dotted and the last *t* crossed.") God knows I've offered a number of such snappy answers in my past books and articles.

But, despite potential problems with ego and their being hackneyed, these are still important questions to answer if you're going to be able to distill your dream into an achievable goal. Your dream of being a knife thrower is moot, for example, if you've very poor eyesight. Well, for your partner's sake at least, I hope it's moot. If you've little patience, odds are you wouldn't be a good kindergarten teacher.

Please understand, I'm not trying shatter a dream you've just started defining. My goal is to help you focus even tighter on the essential elements of your dream. I'd wager that if you're by nature impatient, and you've said your dream is to be a kindergarten teacher, your true dream is probably a variation of the one you've stated; one that isn't as obvious.

Rather than relying on your ability to override your ego, I suggest you also put together a personal focus group. The product on which you're eliciting opinions is you.

Turn to a fresh page, head it FOCUS GROUP, and compile a list of people who you know well and who know you well. Include family and friends, but also coworkers, employers, employees, and clients. Don't rely on those with whom you're currently most comfortable. Reach back to people you worked with years before and forward to acquaintances you've just made. The former are apt to be more brutally honest since they've no longer many vested interests. The opinions of the latter group are interesting because they're a good indication of which of your strengths and weaknesses are the most obvious.

In order to rely on more than just the passage of time to help you elicit honest answers, I suggest you use the following technique. Begin each interview by turning to a fresh page in your notebook, drawing a vertical line down the center of the page, and then asking for positive feedback. Having said some nice things about you, people will feel more comfortable pointing out your less-than-glowing traits. Write down your focus group members' comments, positive or negative, in the lefthand column of the page.

After each interview is complete, try to come up with a reverse spin for each adjective. In other words, take the positive traits or strengths offered and view them in a negative light and take the weaknesses or negative traits noted and spin them positively. For example, if your former boss says you were very "determined," write that trait down in the lefthand column. After the interview, go back to the list and write a synonym with the opposite connotation of the same trait in the righthand column. In this case it might be "stubborn." If your sister says you can be "pushy," write than in the right column, but later write the phrase "proactive" in the opposite column.

Because you're using this list for self analysis rather than self promotion, the way the trait is initially spun by your focus group member matters less than your learning it, acknowledging it, and factoring it into your Second Act. Anyway, odds are there are times in your life when you demonstrate both the positive and negative aspects of the trait.

Go through the list of strengths and weaknesses you've gathered and look for clusters of similar statements. Let's say your wife says that at times you can be "rigid." One of your golfing buddies says you're "dogged." A coworker calls you "tenacious." And, an ex-boss says you were "determined." Write all those descriptions together on a page. Compile as many different clusters as you can and list them on individual pages in your notebook.

If you can, give each cluster a name. The best way to come up with a name is simply to look up the traits in a thesaurus. Try to use a phrase or compound name that expresses the trait as both a strength and a weakness. In the case of those outlined above, perhaps you'd call it persistent/obstinate. Any comments you received that you can't match up with others, which don't seem to fit into a cluster, can be tossed off the list. They represent either a one-time aberration—you just couldn't get enthused about your job as a bank teller—or your very specific reaction to the person interviewed—your childhood friend always knew how to push your buttons and get you mad—rather than a real strength or weakness.

Finally, turn to another fresh page in your notebook and write the following words: "I can be" and then list the names of the clusters.

Dani Identifies Her Strengths and Weaknesses

Dani Kaplan spoke to her parents, siblings, friends, and coworkers about her strengths and weaknesses. Her parents weren't actually that much help. They seemed to be describing the Dani of 20 years ago, rather than the Dani of today. Her two brothers didn't take the exercise very seriously, but her two sisters did. Her older sister—the one in the unhappy marriage—offered only positive descriptions. But her younger sister, a thirty-six-year-old record producer who also lived in New York, was more blunt. Her friends and work peers were diplomatic but did provide some interesting insights.

After compiling the results and browsing through the old *Roget's Thesaurus* that had sat on her bookshelf for years, Dani took out her notebook and wrote, "I can be: confident/vain, ambitious/aggressive, devoted/bossy, and energetic/frantic."

Exercise 3

It's now time for a field trip; just remember to bring your notebook and pen with you. Carve three half-days out of your monthly schedule. They can be on weekends, and they don't need to be consecutive.

On day one, visit the biggest bookstore you can find. Start off by looking at the "new books" sections. What titles and subjects strike your interest? Make notes of the topics and search out the areas of the library or the bookstore that have other books on the subject. Browse the shelves. What other titles interest you? Look at the sections immediately surrounding the area you started where books on related subjects are located. Are there any new subjects that strike you? Follow those leads until you've explored the entire bookstore. Treat yourself to a good cup of coffee at the in-store cafe, and while you're sipping, compile a list of the five or six subjects to which you found yourself most drawn. Write the list on a separate page in your notebook titled INTERESTS.

On day two, head to the largest college library in your area. Go into the stacks, searching for books on each of the subjects you listed earlier. Browse up and down the aisles nearby, seeing the related subjects, making notes of other areas of interest. If you find yourself being drawn to any of these new topics, add them to the list you wrote up at the bookstore.

On day three, take your expanded list of interests to the largest newsstand in your area. (If you can't find a shop with a good collection of periodicals, go back to the college library and go through the periodical section.) Scan the racks of magazines and newspapers looking for periodicals that fit into your areas of interests. If you can, buy a copy of every publication that matches your list. (Alternatively, request the latest copy of every relevant publication from the reference librarian.) Sit down at a comfortable table with your pile of magazines and start skimming them. See what ads and articles strike you. Take notes. Use these new insights to refine the interests you've already listed. For example, if you started off noting you were interested in antiques, refine it to one or two types of antiques, say English country furniture and Civil War weapons.

Turn to another blank page in your notebook. Write the words "I'm interested in" and then write down your refined list.

Dani Sees Where Her Interests Lead

Dani spent three Sunday afternoons in a row developing her list of interests. First she went to the Barnes & Noble store near her apartment. Over a cup of Chai, she wrote that she was drawn to travel, religion/spirituality, photography, entertainment, and ethnic cooking.

Next, rather than going to a college library, she headed to the New York Public Library's Humanities and Social Sciences Branch—the historic library on 42nd Street that used to be the main branch. Looking for areas related to those she'd already singled out, she added art history to her list.

Finally, she headed off to the gigantic newsstand in the lobby of the Met Life Building (formerly the Pan Am Building) to look for publications related to her interests. Although she found some, she wasn't happy with the selection of titles in her areas of interest, which led her back to the library. There, in the periodical room, she found more titles. Looking through the magazines and journals she worked to refine her general interests. She turned to a new page in her diary and wrote, "I'm interested in: European travel, Buddhist meditation, Kabbala, portrait photography, American cinema, and Eastern European cooking."

Exercise 4

With your list of interests complete, give yourself two days relief from self analysis. Refreshed, set aside a couple of hours, find a comfortable chair, and take your notebook. Go back and look at your lists of passions, strengths/weaknesses, and interests. Ask yourself, "What need in me does this passion address?" Perhaps this passion is an expression of one of your strengths or an subconscious effort to conceal a weakness. If you know the need this interest answers, write it down on a page titled NEEDS.

I'm not suggesting that every passion, trait, or interest is the outward manifestation of a deep-seated need. However, many are. Deny that, and you're also denying yourself an excellent opportunity to discover your true dreams and fulfill them.

Let's say you've determined that if you had unlimited funds you'd open a book store. And, perhaps you've figured out you're obsessive and organized. Finally, it's clear that portrait photography is one of your prime interests. What, if anything is underlying those items? The desire to open a bookstore could reflect a need for self education. It's possible your obsessiveness is a response to a need to be in control of your environment. Maybe your interest in portraiture is the manifestation of a need to connect to people. Obviously, this isn't an exact science. Your desire to open a bookstore could represent a need to legitimately own a great many books. Your being organized could come from growing up in a very disorganized household. And, your interest in photo portraiture could stem from a need to find an accurate picture of yourself. Just write down the need you sense or feel *might* be beneath the item on your list. There's no right or wrong answer. All you're looking for are impressions and perceptions.

If you've thought long and hard about one item on your list and can't find an underlying need, don't worry, just move on to the next item. You're not looking for some incredible revelation into your soul or psyche. You're just looking to see whether there just might be some other, perhaps more fundamental dream, hiding under the passion, strength, or interest you've listed. If there is, you might be able to come up with other, perhaps easier ways, to address that need.

Let's say you think needs for control and creativity are underlying your lifelong desire to become a classical pianist. Aren't there other ways to be in control and express your creativity and love of classical music? It's possible running a store selling musical instruments could answer your needs. Maybe starting an online business selling rare classical CDs is the answer. Alternatively, you could become a piano tuner or give piano lessons.

Don't get me wrong. I'm not out to convince you to abandon a lifelong dream or to trim your sails. If you go through all these exercises, and you're more convinced than ever before you want to be a classical pianist, then God bless you, let's go for it. All I'm trying to do is give you as many options as possible to achieve your true dream. I'd be shirking my responsibility if I didn't try to find you the easiest or quickest path there. But if we can't find a shortcut, we'll just need to take the long way.

Dani Looks for the Needs Underlying Her Dreams

Dani thought a great deal about what needs could be underlying her passions, strengths and weaknesses, and interests. She had some ideas, but wanted to get some feedback. I suggested she speak with the younger sister who had been so helpful when coming up with strengths and weaknesses. Dani invited her for dinner and over a bottle of wine they played amateur psychology. In our next conversation, Dani told me some of the needs she thought lay beneath her dreams.

Dani felt that loving to entertain at home and going to the flea market, her interest in Eastern European cooking and Kabbala, and her devotion to others all were probably linked to a need she had to create and maintain family ties and rituals. She had come from a large, closely knit Jewish family that, over the years, had fractured and spread.

Dani said she believed her love of shopping for toys and of FAO Schwartz at Christmas time, and her fond memories of taking her niece to the zoo and of buying her parents a car, all stemmed from a need to nurture.

She felt that the long drives along the ocean, her fond memory of walking the beach at Cape Cod, and her interest in Buddhist meditation might all be linked to a need for some solitude or time alone. When I reminded her that the walk in Cape Cod was with an ex-boyfriend, she laughed and said that when she thinks back to that day his presence was actually incidental.

Finally, Dani thought that her love of shopping for clothing and jewelry, her interest in European travel and places, her memory of being a hit at the award show, and her confidence and, yes, vanity, all came from a need to be attractive and have nice things. She told me that her family always lived beyond their means in order to maintain certain appearances. She and her sister agreed that it was important to both of them to not just be successful but to have the outward trappings of success as well.

Exercise 5

Rather than taking time off, at this point I'd suggest jumping right into the next exercise while your self analysis is still fresh. Get back to that comfortable chair, pull out your now trusty Second Act notebook, and write down what you now perceive your dream to be. I know that's tougher than I've made it sound. Try narrowing it down as much as possible by very narrowly defining your terms and exploring possible options. Let's go through a couple of examples.

You feel your dream is to be a classical pianist. Does that mean you want to play only classical music, no jazz or standards? Think about whether you want to play a grand piano, rather than an upright or an electric keyboard. Do you want to do this for a living, or doesn't it matter if you get paid to play? Consider that this needn't be a full-time job. You could play on weekends only or pursue it just part time. Do you need to be a performer, or would teaching also be acceptable? Perhaps you're only interested in playing solo, or, on the other hand, only want to work with an orchestra or a small group of musicians. Maybe you're not interested in playing anything not of your own choosing. It could be that the location where your playing matters a great deal. Perhaps you only see yourself playing concerts. Or, maybe you'd find it okay to perform at weddings or parties, too. Close your eyes and picture your dream. Do you see yourself playing baroque concerts in churches or afternoon recitals in hotel lobbies?

Perhaps your dream is to have a child. Does that mean you also need to have a spouse? Maybe your real need is to be the mother or father of a child, not necessarily a husband or wife. It could be that you feel an urge to physically give birth to a child. That doesn't always mean you need to have a relationship with the other parent. Do you need to raise the child from infancy? If not, adoption becomes a lot easier. Be honest about all the details. If you feel the child must be the same race as you, don't deny your sentiments. Similarly, think about whether you want just one child, or more.

By asking and answering these kinds of questions you'll be able to make your dream more achievable. I chose these two examples because they illustrate that distilling your dream doesn't mean weakening it. It means boiling it down to its essential elements.

In the case of the dream to be a classical pianist, the more broadly you're willing to define what it means to be a classical pianist, the easier it will be to achieve. Let's say you want to play, not teach. You're not interested in playing jazz or standard, but you're open to doing it part time and in other than concert settings. You're willing to play solo or in a group. This means you could pursue part-time work playing at weddings or parties on your own, as well as looking to join a group of some kind. You could also look for work as an accompanist if you're okay with not picking the music you play.

In the case of wanting to have a child, the more options you're willing to pursue, the easier parenthood becomes. If your goal is strictly to become a parent, then you could become a single parent of an adopted older child of a different race. If your goal is to become a biological parent, you don't need to get married, nor do you even need to have a relationship with the other biological parent or to physically give birth to the child.

Write your distilled dream down on a fresh sheet of paper. Now, distill your prose just as you distilled your ideas. Edit the description down to as few words as possible, making it as clear and specific as you can. Now memorize it. Write this discription in large block letters on its own page in your Second Act notebook, titling the page MISSION STATEMENT. This is what you want to do, what you're going to do, with the rest of your life. It's your opening monologue when you first step out onto the stage of your Second Act.

Dani Distills Her Dream

Dani began thinking about her dream to have a family. While she would like to have a husband, at thirty-nine she didn't know that she could wait to get married to have a child. At this point in her life, she felt her dream of parenting was stronger than her desire for marriage. She knew she wanted to be a mother, but she wasn't sure she felt the need to be pregnant and give birth to her own biological child. There was no man in her life that she felt could be the father. She has friends who had gone through *in vitro* fertilization, and others who had found a donor through a sperm bank. Dani doesn't feel that need. She loves her career and doesn't want to leave it. She felt that if she adopted an older child, it would be easier to arrange for child care. At first she felt she'd prefer a girl to a boy but acknowledged that might only be because she was afraid she'd never find a husband. She decided she doesn't care about the child's gender. She also didn't care about the child's race or ethnic background. "'As long as it's healthy,' was one of my grandmother's favorite expressions," she told me. Dani started writing and editing her dream. Her final result was one simple sentence: "I want to adopt a healthy toddler or young child and continue in my current career." Ironically, it was just about nine months later that Dani did just that.

ARE YOU RARING TO GO, OR READY TO QUIT?

Take a look at your mission statement. What's your reaction to seeing this simple, yet powerful, definition of your deepest held dream?

It could be you're excited, thrilled at the possibility of the glorious life that lies in store for you. You may feel empowered, ready to climb mountains and battle bureaucracies to reach your long-dreamed goal.

On the other hand, it could be you're now convinced you can't possibly do this. Perhaps you think you must have done something wrong in the exercises and should start over again from the beginning. Maybe you're about to put this book down and set aside what you now think is a crazy dream.

Both responses are normal. I've seen people so empowered by distilling their dream they could take on the world. And, I've also seen people so frightened they never went any further in the process. If you've got the bit between your teeth that's great. But if you're hesitant, that's okay too. What you're experiencing is stage fright. It happens to lots of people. I've worked with famous, incredibly successful actors who still feel it before they go before a camera or out on stage for the first time. One well-known film actor once told me the reason actors are notoriously late to a set isn't that they've overslept or are prima donnas—it's that they're scared. I've worked with professional athletes who still feel fear before they step onto the field, ice, or court.

You have a choice.

You can give in to your stage fright, put this book down, and go back to the life you're currently leading. I'll never know and neither will anyone else. You'll be exactly where you were before you started reading. Your dream life will remain locked deep within you, a path never taken, a chance never seized. It will remain, like all fantasies, perfect. But it will still be a fantasy.

Or, you can move on to the next chapter. You can take the leap of faith. You can step up to the plate. You can come out from behind the curtain to take center stage in your Second Act. I need to warn you: Your dream life will no longer be perfect. You'll be faced with having to make choices and compromises and sacrifices in order to reach your goals. But in the end, your dream life will be real. Peter Drucker has written that there are two kinds of risks: "There is the risk you cannot afford to take, and there is the risk you cannot afford not to take." A Second Act is a risk you cannot afford not to take because the payoff is so enormous: You will be creating the life you've always wanted. To do that, however, you need to turn the page.

CHAPTER 3

Developing the
Second Act Mindset

"The call rings up the curtain, always, on a mystery of transfiguration.
The familiar life horizon has been outgrown; the old concepts, ideals and
emotional patterns no longer fit; the time for passing the threshold is
at hand."

—JOSEPH CAMPBELL

I'm proud of you. You were brave enough to make the leap of faith. Now you've raised the curtain on your Second Act. You're on the path to making your dreams real. Your courage will be rewarded by a happier more satisfying life. I guarantee it.[3] Anais Nin once said, "Life shrinks or expands in proportion to one's courage." Well, you've just tripled your life.

It might sound crazy, but believe me, you've just overcome the greatest challenge to having a Second Act. All the techniques for, say, getting an entry-level job at fifty-five, or starting a business at twenty-five, are just that: techniques. They're essential skills and

---

[3] If your Second Act process doesn't result in your being happier and more satisfied, I'll return whatever misery led you to change your life, no questions asked.

tactics, certainly, and, in fact, they take up much of this book. But none of them will be difficult to learn and absorb. It was deciding to step out on stage that was the hard part. The rest is all process.

The start of that process is to develop the right mindset, based on nine building blocks, or principles, I'll be describing in this chapter. Right now, your Second Act consists of a mission statement. Having been distilled to its essential elements, it's a powerful phrase, but it's still just a seedling. Now, we need to prepare the soil so it grows into a mighty tree.

Your open, positive, enthusiastic attitude will be invaluable for your own success. You'll have more energy. Your mind will be sharper. And, you'll be able to react much more quickly. But having the right attitude isn't just of internal importance. It will be essential in your success with the outside world, too. That's because your outside always matches your inside.

If you are feeling good about yourself and secure about what you're doing, you will project that esteem and security. You'll stand a little straighter. You'll unconsciously smile warmly. Your eyes will be bright and focused like a laser. If you are feeling unsure and insecure, that lack of esteem will come across loud and clear. You'll either mope around as if you're pulling a ton of bricks or nervously dart about like a chipmunk. You'll have a perpetual scowl on your face, or you'll sport an obviously phony grin. You'll be unable to make or maintain direct eye contact.

I believe success and failure can be self-fulfilling prophecies. Feel like you're too old to actually go back to college, and you'll broadcast that, making the admissions director think you might not be a good candidate, and as a result, reducing your chances. Feel like you can launch a business at age twenty-six with little experience, and your confidence will be contagious, convincing the lender you're going to be the next Bill Gates, maximizing your chances of getting the loan.

What's the mindset that best allows a Second Act to flourish? I can't characterize or define it with one word or even a short phrase. It's not something I read in any philosophical treatise, absorbed from a self-help seminar, or heard in a religious sermon. It's a set of nine building blocks or principles I've been preaching and refining and living for more than twenty-five years. They've worked for hundreds of people, whether they were married seniors or single twenty somethings, wealthy actors or working class masons. They worked for me, too.

Looking back on my own Second Act, so much of it seems serendipitous. I do indeed feel I have been blessed—that's one reason I've spent my life since trying to empower other people. I also believe in a higher power. But, I don't believe God spent all those years looking out for me personally and arranging for one thing to lead to another. I have a very healthy ego, but I don't think I'm that important. The blessings I received aren't unique. Instead, I believe opportunities of this kind are placed around everyone. It was thanks to my attitude that I was able to see those opportunities and was willing to go after them.

How do I know these opportunities surround you? Well, when I began my life coaching practice, much of what I did was tell people how I reinvented myself and suggest they adopt the same attitude I brought to the process. I discovered it worked for them. . . all of them. Honestly: Everyone I've worked with who adopted these nine building blocks to an open, positive attitude and was willing to go through the process outlined in the rest of this book has had a successful Second Act.

HOW I REINVENTED MYSELF

If you recall from Chapter 1, I was struck ill at the age of 48. However, having been diagnosed with tuberculosis rather than lung cancer, I felt like I'd been given a second chance at life. I was grateful to God for having spared me. On the other hand, I was frightened. My family and I had been placed in a precarious position. I had no job. My wife, Corky, had no job. We had a big mortgage. We had outstanding loans to help pay for my son to attend a very expensive private college. We had outstanding loans to help pay for my three daughters attending private high schools. It wasn't until my wife expressed faith in our future that I began to feel some hope return. I started to raise the curtain.

Actually, my wife, Corky, was the first to pull on the ropes, taking a job as an assistant at *New York*.[4] She had just gotten her master's degree before I got sick and had planned to become a teacher now that all our children were in high school. However, the job at the magazine paid better, and we needed the money.

I swallowed by pride and borrowed $500 each from two friends, Bob Farquah, a builder from Watertown, NY, and David Pierez, an attorney, to give me a little bit of a financial cushion. Knowing banking and lending, I made calls to all my creditors and worked out deals so we could make reduced payments.

After a few months, the medications I was taking started to work. I felt my strength returning. I called a good friend of mine from the bank, Bill Davidson, and asked for his help in developing a resume. In the course of compiling the information, he reminded me I was a lawyer. It sounds crazy, but I had been a real estate developer, venture capitalist, and banker for so long that I had stopped thinking of myself as an attorney, even though I'd graduated law school, passed the bar, and had been in practice for a few years. He also taught me how to categorize my eclectic

---

[4] Corky spent nineteen years at *New York*, most as the editor of her own column called "Best Bets." In 2001, rather than resting on her laurels or thinking of retirement, she launched yet another Second Act, becoming style director of *Gourmet*.

business experience into terms human resource people in business would understand: marketing, management, and finance.

Resume finished, I started networking and sending it out to prospects. I came up with what, at the time, I thought was a brilliant idea. I developed a list of companies that had been in the Fortune 500 in the prior year, but this year had dropped ten or more spots. I wrote the CEO of each telling him (at the time they were all men) I was a brilliant turnaround specialist who knew how to bring his company back. I also gave copies of my resume to everyone I knew.

Of course, I got no response to my turnaround campaign. The CEOs probably didn't like being reminded of their failings, and the last person they would have looked to for help was an out-of-work wise guy. I did get a bite from my networking, however. But from an unexpected area.

Jim Casey, an accountant friend of mine, had given my resume to Joe Frey, the chairman of the business department at Marymount Manhattan College. He was struck by my unusual background and called. It seemed he needed an adjunct professor to teach a course in advertising over the summer and asked whether I'd be interested. Seeing I had four teenage children, he said I must know how to communicate to college students.

This was like asking an amateur violinist if he wanted to perform at Carnegie Hall. You see, I had a reverence for higher education. That's because I had never gotten a bachelor's degree myself. I was accepted at Brooklyn Law School after only two years of college. Already in a rush to be a success, I grabbed at the chance. I got my law degree, but in the process I missed out on all sorts of coursework that would have made me a more well-rounded person.[5]

---

[5] I eventually did go back and get my bachelor's degree. . . at the age of fifty-eight.

I jumped at the offer of a teaching job, not just because I was enthralled with the idea of being a professor, but because I desperately needed the money.

There were three problems. First, I was scared because I had never taught before. I knew I could communicate in front of small groups, but I had never lectured to a room full of people. Second, I knew almost nothing about advertising. And third, despite having four teens, I really wasn't an expert at communicating with kids.[6] The only teen I could really communicate with was also the only person I knew who had any knowledge of higher education: my son Michael. I called to ask his advice.

He suggested I pick up a couple of advertising textbooks and read them cover to cover to learn the jargon and conventional theories. He suggested I just treat the students like adults—they'd be flattered. Finally, he told me that students love interesting independent projects and suggested I teach advertising, not just by lecturing, but by having the students develop a real-world advertising campaign. Jimmy Carter was running for reelection at the time, so, putting two and two together, I had the class work up ad campaigns for him.

The chairman of the department thought this was terrific. Eager to promote the school and his department, he made some calls to explain what my class was doing. The advertising columnist of *The New York Times* picked up on the story. Carter advisers saw the piece and invited the class to present their campaigns. Of course, that made even more news.

The college was thrilled with all the publicity and asked me to teach another course the next semester. Rather than pushing my

---

[6] All four of my children have grown up to become wonderful and very successful adults. Whenever people ask me for my parenting secrets I tell them to speak to Corky. . . I had nothing to do with it.

luck I decided to tackle a subject I actually knew a lot about: credit.

During that first summer of teaching I became friendly with another adjunct professor. Gregor Roy was a fascinating character. A former soldier in the Scots Guards and then a headmaster of a Scottish public (what here would be called, private) school, Gregor had come to America at forty-five in an effort to become an actor. He was getting bit parts on Broadway and in television but was paying his rent by teaching English at the college. Because we were both odd birds in the faculty lounge, we naturally gravitated together and became friendly.

One day when I was home working on my next lecture and scanning the help-wanted ads, Gregor stopped by. He was upset and frightened. Two months before he had a medical emergency that set him back financially. In that day's mail he had received threatening letters from the telephone company and his landlord. He was terrified. In typically odd Gregor fashion he was more concerned with his telephone than having a roof over his head. "If they cut off my telephone, I won't be able to get a call if I'm offered a part. I could miss my big chance."

I calmed Gregor down and told him I could help. I took his bills, picked up my telephone, and started making calls. Knowing what language creditors wanted to hear, and that I could "push the up button" whenever I reached a roadblock, I was able to work out payment plans for Gregor's telephone and rent in less than an hour. After all, I had done this for Corky and I not too long before. When I had finished, Gregor stared at me wide-eyed, mouth agape. "This is amazing," he said. "You must let people know this is possible and how they can do it. You must write about his." I told him I didn't know how to write. He said he did and would help me.

For the next two months he and I labored over a manuscript, with me dictating and Gregor taking notes, returning the next day

with a handwritten text on yellow legal pads. When we had something we thought presentable I asked Corky to show it to a friend
she'd made at *New York*: Debbie Harkins, the very well-respected
executive editor of the magazine.

Debbie was able to see past the amateurish submission and
spot the germ of a good article. She helped Gregor and I rework
the idea and the piece until it became a short service article that
ran in *New York* called "How to Get a Loan from a Balky
Banker."

With some success coming from unusual places, I was beginning
to feel better about myself. Improved spirits helped improve my
physical health, too. I soon felt well enough to be open to the idea
when people began to call me for advice on their credit problems.
At first, these consultations were just another source of income,
supplementing the small stipend I was getting from teaching.

Seeing there was a real need for good credit advice, I started
teaching an adult ed. course on fixing your credit through the
Learning Annex. Because I was still feeling a bit weak, I'd have
the students come to my apartment for one weekly two-hour session. At first the sessions were draining and sad. I saw them as
nothing more than a way to make some desperately needed
money. But over time I began to find real joy in helping other
people overcome their problems.

My credit classes had become fairly popular, and as a result I
got a call one day from a young radio host named Dean Shepherd.
He asked me whether I wanted to work with him on a series of
shows on consumer credit. Having long harbored a childhood
dream of being a radio personality (yes, I'm that old), I jumped at
the chance.

Dean and I did three shows together. They seem to be received
very well. A literary agent heard the shows, found out about my
teaching credit and offering consultations, and went back to read
my article in *New York*. She thought she'd be able to sell a book

by me about credit. Once again I was thrilled. I was as impressed by writers as I was college professors. I thought Gregor would be thrilled as well. I was wrong. Gregor was afraid that if he was writing he'd be unavailable when that big call came from a casting director. Meanwhile, the agent succeeded in selling the book idea to Simon and Schuster and I was now contracted to write a book called *How To Borrow Money*. Once again I turned to my son Michael for help. He introduced me to two college friends of his who were willing to work with me on the project.

While working with Michael's two friends was difficult, the book turned out to strike a cord. A producer at *Good Morning America* read it and agreed to book me on the show.

I remember that morning like it was yesterday. It was almost three years to the day that I'd learned I had tuberculosis, not cancer. My life had gone in directions I'd never anticipated. My family was still struggling financially, but I could see a light at the end of the tunnel. I found myself in the bathroom at ABC Television in New York, nervously waiting to go on television. I went into a stall and got down on my knees, not to vomit but to pray. I prayed to God, not offering thanks, or asking for success, but begging that I don't make a fool of myself. I didn't. The host who interviewed me, a very young woman just starting out named Joan Lunden, put me at ease.

My appearance on *Good Morning America* led to many more consulting clients, not just wanting help with cleaning up their credit, but also looking for help in borrowing to buy homes. Meanwhile, a marketing executive at American Express had seen me on television, found out I had taught at colleges, and thought I'd be a good person to travel around America for them, speaking to college students about smart credit.

Being on the road for American Express meant I needed help with my growing base of clients. I was introduced to a young woman named Jane Morrow, who had been working at the

Federal Reserve Bank. She had decided to go back to law school but was looking for work that would fit in with her school schedule. She agreed to come work with me.

Having seen the powerful impact articles and books could have on my life, I decided to try to write more. Of course, that meant I needed a writer. A client introduced me to a young magazine editor named Mark Levine who was looking to break out of editing and into writing. We hit it off and began working together.

With the benefit of hindsight, that was the moment when the curtain fully rang up on the Second Act of my life. Jane and Mark were the final pieces that helped me to create a legal consulting and life coaching business, that today, almost twenty-five years later, continues to provide me with a good living and incredible emotional and psychological satisfaction.

It has also given me the opportunity to teach others the lessons I'd learned. The most important of those lessons, I now believe, was that you can live two lives in one lifetime; that you can have a Second Act.

THE NINE BUILDING BLOCKS
FOR A SECOND ACT

As I wrote earlier, everyone I've worked with for almost twenty-five years who adopted my nine building blocks to an open, positive attitude and who was willing to do the projects outlined in the rest of this book has had a successful Second Act.

After making that kind of claim you might think the attitude I'm suggesting is unique, some kind of special secret formula. On the contrary, the principles I learned and now preach aren't rare insights. The building blocks I'm suggesting you adopt for your psychological and emotional foundation aren't exotic. In fact, I'm sure you'll find many of them familiar. But believe me, their

---

JACKIE MASON

Jackie Mason had little choice about his first act. His great-great grandfather, great-grandfather, grandfather, father, and three brothers were all rabbis. Mason, born in Sheboygan, Wisconsin, and raised on Manhattan's Lower Eastside, followed suit. He began as a cantor and then, at the age of twenty-five, was ordained a rabbi. But, despite the family tradition, Mason felt the need for a Second Act. At the age of 28, he quit his synagogue and raised the curtain on his Second Act, setting out to become a professional comedian saying, "Someone in the family had to make a living." After some notable early television successes, Mason's career stagnated until he launched a one man broadway show called *The World According to Me.* A smash hit, it was followed by a world tour and four subsequent broadway shows: *Jackie Mason: Politically Incorrect, Love Thy Neighbor, Jackie Mason: Brand New,* and *Much Ado About Everything.* ■

---

ubiquity doesn't make them any less true. I've learned you don't need to reinvent the wheel to reinvent your life.

Parenthetically, I'll be offering some short examples of how these building blocks can be used or are expressed in a Second Act. Please don't feel short changed by their brevity—I'll get into far more detail of that kind in the second part of the book. For now, however, I didn't want you to get bogged down in nitty-gritty tactics when you're trying to adopt new, general attitudes.

BUILDING BLOCK 1

Reach Out for Help . . . and Give It Back in Return.

Everyone needs help some time. Having to ask others for assistance doesn't mark you as being weak or having failed. It just means you're human. Don't let false pride stand in the way of your dreams coming true. The world is too complex for any one person to know, or be skilled at, everything. Life is too ambiguous to rely just on your own perception and perspective. Getting others to help you increases your odds of success by allowing you to leverage your time and abilities. It's also a wonderful way to turn someone who could see himself as an adversary or competitor into a friend or ally.

That's what Peter Douglas, a program director at a Midwestern radio station discovered. The curly-haired, bearded forty-six year old, needed to spin his radio experience so investors would be more apt to help him start the online jazz record store of his dreams. Peter turned to the owner of the local music store and the manager of the nearby giant bookseller's music department for help. Not only did the two willingly help, but the three music entrepreneurs now meet for lunch once a month to discuss trends in the industry.

I've found the key to getting people to help you is simply to ask. I've helped people plan out dialogs for thousands of different conversations and negotiations.[7] In the process I've found the single most effective icebreaker is "I have a problem, and I'm hoping you can help me with it."

Along with being open to asking for help, provide it generously. I firmly believe if you help others you will be helped in turn.

---

[7] I've even written and edited books on the subject: Mark Levine's and my own *Lifescripts*, *Lifescripts for Employees*, *Lifescripts for the Self Employed*, and *Lifescripts for Managers*; and *Lifescripts for Friends and Family* by Erik Kolbell.

If, let's say, you're thinking of going back to college after years in the job market, the admissions officer at a college could become an obstacle. But, what if you send her an email, introducing yourself, noting your past successes, and ask to meet with her for advice. Everyone loves to be asked for advice. When you meet her, portray yourself as someone looking for a mentor. Ask her about the challenges returning students face. Find out whether there are any departments particularly open to older students. As the conversation progresses, you can become more specific, for example, asking whether it's possible to avoid having to take the GRE exams, for instance. You can ask for her help in selecting an advisor or setting up meetings with professors. By asking for help and developing a relationship, you can turn a gatekeeper into a mentor.

BUILDING BLOCK 2

Embrace Conflicting Needs . . . Don't Settle.

It's human nature to try to split the difference: to look for some middle ground or half-way point between what appear to be opposing points. That's true in everything from negotiating the purchase of a home to launching a Second Act. The problem with such an approach is you'll never actually get what you want; you'll always settle for less. Let's say you want independence and security. A compromise leaves you with neither.

Instead, be open to moving from one pole to another throughout your life. Accept that there will always be tension and change. You can opt for a secure life, but after ten years of security perhaps you feel the need for a change. Then jump to the other extreme of independence. A life led strictly down the middle may never leave you low, but neither will it raise you up.

Taking a job inside an dynamic organization that encourages its employees to be innovative and creative may seem to satisfy your

JOHN TESH

From early in his childhood John Tesh loved music. Raised in Garden City, New York, Tesh played piano and trumpet from the age of six. In high school he was named to the New York State Symphonic Orchestra. But rather than study music, Tesh went to North Carolina State University and became a communications major. He earned his degree in 1975 and began pursuing a broadcasting career. Working in local television news, he progressively worked in Nashville, Raleigh, and Orlando. At twenty-three he became the youngest reporter at New York's WCBS TV. After winning two local Emmy awards and an AP award for investigative journalism, Tesh joined CBS Sports. While reporting on the Tour de France in 1982, he

entrepreneurial urge as well as your need for security. But dynamic organizations don't often provide all that much security. And, no amount of in-house innovation will ever truly satisfy an entrepreneur. A better approach might be to spend a few years running your own business, preceded or followed by a period working as an employee of an established and stable organization.

That's the approach Peter Hamilton has chosen to follow. The lanky thirty-seven year old has been a successful freelance journalist, based out of his native Chicago, for more than a decade. Tired of the constant hustle and insecurity, he fought off the impulse to compromise and look for a full-time journalism job and instead landed a corporate communications spot with an insurance company.

offered to compose original music to underscore the coverage. Viewers began contacting the network, asking where they could buy tapes of the music. Tesh started selling cassettes from his garage. In 1986 he was named host of *Entertainment Tonight*, but continued composing theme music for sporting events, including "Roundball Rock" for the NBA, which became NBC's signature music. For 10 years he worked on his music while maintaining his broadcasting career, winning awards in both the New Age and Jazz categories. In 1995, a video of his concert performance—"Live at Red Rocks"— became one of the most successful fundraising programs for PBS. The album from the concert went gold, and the video went double platinum. No longer able to resist the pull of the Second Act he'd been keeping on the back burner since high school, Tesh left *Entertainment Tonight* in 1996 to concentrate on his music career. ■

BUILDING BLOCK 3

Cast Lots of Irons in the Fire.

You never know which opportunity will work out or where it could lead. And, you can never count on any one particular hope panning out. That's why it's essential you explore every avenue that comes your way. Going on an interview for a job you're not really interested in could lead to another open position.

For example, I never thought of teaching at a university as a career option when I lost my job at the bank. But when the chance came along I followed up on it, and it became the first step in my Second Act.

There's no such thing as having too many choices. Don't be afraid of multiple things panning out. You'll then be able to choose between opportunities. Or, you'll have so many opportunities you'll need to enlist help. Those are things to celebrate, not fear.

For instance, don't worry about approaching multiple acting coaches if you're thinking of pursuing a Second Act on the stage. What's the worst that could happen? If more than one expresses an interest in taking you on as a student you're in the wonderful position of being able to pick and choose between them. Suddenly you're the one who's in demand.

When Rodney Albert, a distinguished fifty-three year old Congregationalist minister in New York decided to launch a Second Act outside the clergy, he cast out scores of feelers. They, in turn, led him to explore previously unforeseen directions. One of which he found fascinating. The former minister is now a vice president of sales with a major auction house.

BUILDING BLOCK 4

Go through Open Doors.

When an opportunity presents itself, take advantage. In order to launch a Second Act, you must be willing to take chances. When you go through an open door you're not heading toward a dead end. There are no dead ends in life. Who knows, there may not even be a dead end in death. Whichever door you go through, rest assured there will be others later on.

Don't be afraid of defeats—those are the best learning experiences. Failure only comes from standing still. Looking back on life from the wisdom of experience, it's the risks not taken, the open doors not entered, that lead to regrets. No one on their death bed has ever said "I should have taken fewer chances in life."

In my case, it turned out that counseling people with poor credit wasn't the financially savviest approach to consulting and life coaching. Let's be frank: They already had shown themselves to be unreliable customers. But, it was through credit counseling that I started getting real estate clients, who then became career clients, and business clients, and so on.

Marie Purcell, thirty-seven, and Jean Lemaire, forty-three, were happy with their careers as documentary filmmakers and with their marriage. Their dream Second Act was to move out of the city to lead a more bucolic life in the country. They were just in the early stages of planning their Second Act when they discovered a 110-year-old farm house for sale in Central New York. They didn't hesitate to go through the open door—they bought it.

BUILDING BLOCK 5

Don't Be Ashamed of Talents or Shortcomings . . . . Be Candid.

Some people find other's self denigration to be admirable. My guess is that's only because it gives their own egos more room to expand. If you rely on your assets and attributes coming to light on their own over the course of time, you'll never have a Second Act. You might not even have a first. If you don't promote your own talents, probably no one else will.

For years, Stephanie Wexler cultivated humility. The forty-four-year-old energetic wife and mother always belittled her photography hobby and hesitated to submit her works to either contests or local galleries. But when it came time to launch her Second Act, she forced herself to become comfortable with self promotion.

Besides being open to blowing your own horn, don't hesitate to admit a lack of understanding or knowledge. That demonstrates candor, not stupidity, and that's a valuable trait in launching a

Second Act. Odds are you'll be changing direction in your Second Act. Your success won't be based on having comprehensive knowledge but on character and general background. Pretend to know something you don't, and you've demonstrated a character flaw. Candidly admit a gap in knowledge, and your character takes on new luster. If you have nothing to say, say nothing.

The world is filled with people trying to be something or someone they're not. If in your Second Act you want to meet a life partner, it's better to be completely yourself than to adopt an artificial persona. It may take longer to meet someone, but when you do you'll know any attraction is genuine and will be long term.

BUILDING BLOCK 6

Practice Bifocal Vision.

One of the keys to a Second Act is learning how to mitigate risks. You do that by practicing bifocal vision: focusing on both the present and the future at the same time. For example, maintaining your expertise in your current career while simultaneously adding new skills for your next career. The idea is to keep both short and long terms in mind. In my experience it's a very rare situation when you actually need to give up one for the other. Such a false sacrifice is more indicative of a lack of self confidence than anything else.

Choosing a bird in the hand over two in the bush means you're afraid you won't be able to catch those two who are still free. Letting the one in your hand go in order to pursue the two who are still free means you're afraid this is the only time you'll ever find two birds in the bush—that this chance came by luck. The answer is to shift the bird from your hand to your pocket and use both hands to go after the other two.

For example, do everything you can so your boss at the accounting firm falls in love with your work all over again—just as he did when he first hired you. That way you'll have plenty of time to find that job in the entertainment industry. If you're offered a raise or promotion by your current boss, take it. It's a sign your renewed vows are being reciprocated. But don't stop looking for a new job as well.

Attorney Ben Bacon, a brawny fifty-five year old, could read the handwriting on the wall. His company had been acquired by a firm with its own legal department. But rather than give up, Ben cultivated his new superiors even while he made plans to open his own office. He accepted a promotion just three months before tendering his resignation. And, his second client was the firm he left.

BUILDING BLOCK 7

Just Row . . . and Leave the Steering to God.

We are all unique individuals. Our journeys are all different. In order to succeed in your Second Act, you need to let go of the tiller and concentrate instead on the oars. Don't try to predict your path though life. Second acts are rarely straight lines or steady climbs up ladders; they are unique journeys into your heart and soul. Just put one foot in front of the other. There is no such thing as wasted movement or going in the wrong direction.

Jane Parker, a gamine-like thirty-seven year old, has learned to trust God's navigation. She has gone from undergraduate English major in Florida, to waitress in Europe, to MBA student in California, to international marketing consultant. Her circuitous path seems to have led her to her dream Second Act: She's now assistant headmaster of a private prep school in Connecticut.

Famous Second Act

JOHN LE CARRÉ

After graduating from Oxford in 1956, David Cornwell tried a number of different jobs including teaching German at Eton. Finally, in 1960 he joined the British Foreign Office (the equivalent of the State Department), and due to his fluency in German, was sent to serve as second secretary at the British embassy in Bonn, West Germany. In his spare time, he began penning mystery novels under a pseudonym, because members of the Foreign Office were not supposed to publish under their own names. In 1963 his third novel, *The Spy Who Came in from the Cold,* became a bestseller, winning numerous awards and eventually being made into a film starring Richard Burton. Thanks to the book's success, the thirty-three-year-old Cornwell was able to resign from his job and start writing full time. Under the name John le Carré he has written more than 18 novels, several of which have been turned into major films and television miniseries. In the process, his work has transcended the espionage and mystery genres and is know seen as an exploration of the modern human condition. ■

As a control freak myself, I know how hard it is to not plan out your life ahead of time. But I've learned, and keep reminding myself, that time spent worrying about what might happen or what could go wrong is less efficient in the long run than time spent actually doing something.

If your Second Act could potentially involve a move to another location, don't start investigating movers, new schools for your children, and scanning real estate ads before you even get started. Just do what you need to do to launch your Second Act and allow the developments to naturally unfold over time. If at some point you discover you need to relocate, then you can start addressing those concerns. But until that point, don't set up roadblocks. You'll waste time and energy addressing problems that may just be ungrounded fears.

BUILDING BLOCK 8

Embrace Your Incomparability.

You are one of a kind. There is no one else exactly like you. No one else has dreams and hopes identical to your own. No one else comes from where you came, stands where you stand right now, or will end up where you end up. That's why it doesn't make sense to compare your success or progress to anyone else's or to some external schedule or checklist drafted to fit some nonexistent average life.

Sarah Bennett, a twenty-six-year-old computer game designer living in San Francisco is working hard at embracing her incomparability. While her job is exciting and challenging she feels it has left her social life in a state of arrested development. Most of her friends are marrying, and a few are starting families. Still, while developing her Second Act, she's focusing on not comparing her progress to others.

Sometimes people tell me they're sorry they didn't come to see me sooner for advice. I always correct them, saying they came at just the right time. If they came sooner, they might not have been ready to hear what I was saying. The same is true of you: You are reading this book at exactly the right time. You picked it up at the moment when you are best prepared to launch your Second Act. You are just where you should be right now; just where you are supposed to be. As John Lennon sang, "There isn't anywhere you can be that isn't where you were meant to be."

You may not be in a comfortable place, but that doesn't mean it's not the right place. Just because you're called to follow a certain path, doesn't mean it will be an easy journey. To get to a mountain top you've got to climb, sometimes over rocky and difficult terrain.

Try to banish the concept of losers from your view of yourself and others. Life isn't a zero sum game or a race in which there is only one winner and lots of losers. Others' successes do not diminish you, and your achievements and victories don't diminish them. We can all be winners if we become who we truly want to be. Launch your Second Act, and you're a winner.

On his deathbed the great Hasidic master Rabbi Zusya of Hanipol said, "In the coming world, they will not ask me, 'Why were you not like Moses?' They will ask me, 'Why were you not what you, Zusya, could have been?'"

BUILDING BLOCK 9

The Keystone—Have Hope in the Future.

For me, the single most important element in the Second Act attitude—the keystone that holds all the other building blocks together into a solid foundation—is this: Believe good things will happen, and they will. Have hope in the future, and you'll be able to spot the potential good in a situation, or see the opportunity amidst the danger. Look for blessings, and you'll spot them. I'm not suggesting you become a Pollyanna. You wouldn't be human if you didn't get shocked, sad, or angry. Vent your heart or spleen if you need to. But don't give in to darkness. I believe there's always light. As Sophocles wrote: "Look and you will find it—what is unsought will go undetected."

Losing a job, for instance, is always traumatic. But many times I've seen job loss free someone to pursue opportunities they would not have otherwise. The short-term pain often turns into a better job or career, or a happier life, long term.

We in Western cultures believe pain, anguish, or fear over a situation or circumstance implies it's a tragedy waiting to happen. But in Eastern philosophies, pain and fear are viewed differently. Buddhism and Taoism, for example, focus on the duality of life. They teach that you cannot have good without there also being evil; that without experiencing pain, you'll never experience pleasure. They also teach that these matched pairs of extremes are so inexorably linked that sometimes it's hard to tell one from the other.

A classic example is the old Chinese story of the horse that ran away. It's been told many times in many different ways, so I'll just offer it in a nutshell.

In a small village in rural China lives a poor but wise farmer. One day his only horse runs away. His neighbors come by to offer their sympathy, saying what a terrible misfortune. All the wise farmer says is "perhaps." The next day the missing horse returns, leading back with him an entire herd of wild horses. The neighbors come by to celebrate, saying how wonderful. All the wise farmer says is "perhaps." The next day the farmer's only son goes to tame one of the wild horses, and in the process, breaks his leg. The neighbors all come by to commiserate, saying how awful it is. All the wise farmer says is "perhaps." The next day the forces of the local warlord come to town to forcibly impress all the young men of the village and lead them to war. Because of his fractured leg, the farmer's only son is left behind. Again the neighbors come by to offer congratulations. All the wise farmer says is "perhaps."

The moral I take from the story is that all situations, no matter how terrible they appear on the surface, have within them the seeds and possibility of some good.

This is even expressed in language. A famous example is that the Chinese symbol for the word "crisis" is made up of two characters: one meaning "danger" and the other meaning "opportunity." A less known, but equally telling, linguistic example is that the root for the word "crisis" is the Greek "krinein" which means "turning point."

Understanding that a crisis offers an opportunity in no way diminishes pain you might be experiencing right now, or minimizes fear you could be feeling. I'm simply suggesting pain and fear could actually be yet another signal it's time to pursue a Second Act. In fact, historically, many Second Acts have been prompted by physical, financial, emotional, or psychological crises.

You may feel powerless, but you're not: With the right attitude, you can reinvent yourself. Having gotten the building blocks and the right mind set in place, your next step is to identify the obstacles you're facing.

CHAPTER 4

Identifying Closed Doors

"It is very rare that you meet with obstacles in this world which the humblest man has not faculties to surmount."

—HENRY DAVID THOREAU

There's nothing more terrifying than the unknown. Think back to the times you were most scared while watching a movie. I'll bet they were at moments when someone up on the screen was about to open a closed door, or step into a darkened tunnel, or turn a corner. Ironically, the anticipation of the horrors that could suddenly appear were always far more frightening than whatever actually did show up. Films like *Jaws* or *The Blair Witch Project*, for example, are so successful because they spend more time letting us dream up our own fears from what remains unknown and unseen, rather than actually showing us something.

Right now the obstacles to a Second Act are at their most daunting because they're still nameless and shapeless. They're like closed doors, blocking your path, hiding innumerable imagined traps and terrors. I've been there. I know what that's like. When obstacles are abstract it's easy to start playing out worst-case scenarios in your head. As a result, general, free-form fears and problems seem insurmountable.

To make matters worse, some people find going through the kinds of exercises outlined in this book frightening. Although to many this soul searching is empowering, it's not uncommon for feelings of vulnerability to suddenly crop up. That's nothing to be ashamed of. You began this journey knowing the life you were leading—your first act—wasn't working in one way or another. You were courageous enough to define the life of your dreams and to put yourself in the right frame of mind. But while you can now visualize the end result, the path to get there is still unknown, and to some people, that's very frightening. They feel they're not who they used to be, but they're not yet who they want to be. They're in a scary sort of limbo.

Writers and philosophers have all sorts of names for this uncomfortable place. Some call it the "dark night of the soul." Others name it the "night sea journey" or the "descent into hell." Personally, I think of it as standing alone on a darkened stage. You've summoned up the courage to step out from behind the curtain, but you can't see the audience, and you still don't know your lines.

The urge to run off the stage is probably pretty strong. Even though we know the life we were leading was in some ways unsatisfying, it's at least known. That makes it comfortable. There's that old saying, "Better the devil you know than the devil you don't know." We all know people who have been in this kind of place and have turned back: the woman whose relationship is unsatisfying, perhaps even toxic, but who stays in it rather than leave; the man who despises his job, and complains endlessly, but won't look for another.

Whenever I've faced this kind of situation in my life, I've always responded the same way: I get out from between my own ears and I start making a list. I suppose it's the control freak in me coming out. Facing the unknown, I instinctively try to make it familiar. Confronting the abstract, I try to make it concrete. Whenever I confront what seems a monumental task, I break it down into bite-size pieces that I can handle in a step-by-step manner. In this situation, that means clearly identifying all the barriers between you and the life of your dreams. This works both for those empowered by the future and for those frightened by it.

THE TWELVE MOST COMMON CLOSED DOORS

The specifics of the obstacles you face will be unique because both you and the life of your dreams are unique. For instance, an unemployed fifty-two-year-old man who has spent his working life as an advertising executive, but who now wants to be a novelist, is facing different hurdles than the thirty-year-old woman who wants to leave her job as an elementary school teacher and become a stay-at-home mom. And, while their dreams aren't all that different, she is facing different obstacles than the thirty-nine-year-old woman who wants to start a family but keep her job.

Unfortunately, in the pages of this book it's not possible for me to address these obstacles in a very specific manner. I wish I could, and I invite you to write me if you find that the general advice I offer in the remainder of this book isn't sufficient.[8] Later in this chapter I will, of course, be offering you some exercises so you can come up with your own personal list of specific obstacles. Until then, I ask your indulgence while I make some generalizations.

In the three decades I've been helping people launch Second Acts I've found there are twelve general obstacles: age, money,

---

[8] You can write me care of HarperCollins, 10 East 53rd Street, New York, NY 10022, or better yet, email me at spollan@wbcsk.com.

GEORGE FOREMAN

When George Foreman first won boxing's heavyweight championship by knocking out Joe Frazier in 1973, he was a lean, sullen twenty-four year old. After losing his title to Muhammad Ali in one of boxing's greatest upsets, his career began sinking. After losing another fight in 1977, Foreman experienced a religious awakening, retired from boxing, and was ordained a minister. He established his own church and began counseling prisoners and troubled youth. In 1987, after a ten-year absence, Foreman returned to the ring, but this time as an overweight, forty plus, fun-loving every man. Incredibly, he won the heavyweight championship again by beating Michael

duration, consent, location, physical condition, education and training, timing, esteem, fear of failure, fear of success, and fatalism. Let's go over them individually.

1. *Age*: In my experience, this is the most common barrier cited. That's because it cuts both ways, and as a result, impacts everyone. Most often, people believe they're too old to pursue the life of their dreams. They'll tell me, "I'm forty-five years old. Who's going to hire me to become a junior editor at a publishing company?" But there are also times when people think they're too young to succeed at their chosen Second Act. It's not unusual for people to say something like, "I'm only twenty-six. No one is going to lend someone my age money to start a bookstore."

Moorer in 1994. But Foreman's real Second Act began when he was introduced to a table-top grilling appliance by Salton. Foreman, enthusiastic about the product and the way it cooked his favorite food—hamburgers—thought of purchasing the rights, but then realized he needed marketing and distribution expertise. He approached Salton, suggested increasing the size and altering the design, and offered to go into partnership with them. The rest is marketing history. Foreman's Second Act as a television pitchman was far more lucrative than his boxing career. More than ten million of the grills have been sold, and Foreman has pocketed more than $50 million in royalties. In 2002, Salton bought Foreman out of his royalty agreement and purchased nonexclusive lifetime use of his name and image for $137.5 million in cash and stock. ■

2. *Money*: A very close second in frequency is the worry that either you don't have sufficient financial reserves to launch a Second Act, or that pursuing your dream life won't offer enough of an income to keep you and your family afloat. People who believe their savings aren't up to the transition generally say something like, "We're just scraping by now. We don't have the savings for me to go back to school right now." Those who aren't convinced their Second Act will provide a living wage express it by saying something like, "I've got a mortgage, two car loans, and a daughter about to go to college. I can't leave the corporate world and take a 40 percent pay cut to become a high school teacher."

3. *Duration*: Second acts often consist of dramatic transitions requiring a few steps backwards before moving forward again. As a result, you might be concerned by the amount of time you think it will take to succeed in your new life. One forty-three-year-old entrepreneur who wanted to change his career said to me, "It will take a minimum of three years for me to a get a law degree and then pass the bar exam. And that's going to school full time. I don't have that kind of time."

4. *Consent*: No man or woman is an island. Regardless of age, gender, or marital status, you may find you need the consent, and perhaps even outright support, of someone else to pursue your dream. It's common to fear consent will be withheld or support won't be forthcoming. The usual expression of this fear that I hear comes from women, deals with both consent and support, and goes something like this, "My husband won't want me to give up my job and stay home with a baby. And I just know he wouldn't split the child care chores with me so I could work outside the home, too." That being said, I've also had married men tell me their wives wouldn't accept their shifting to a lesser earning career, and singles of both sexes express worry over how parents would react to their Second Acts.

5. *Location*: Despite all the advances in information and communication technologies and all the moves toward a globally connected economy, people often believe they're simply not living in the right location to lead the life of their dreams. This obstacle is most often cited by people whose Second Act involves a career that has historically been associated with one or a handful of specific locations. I've had people tell me, "To become a successful actor you

must live in New York or Los Angeles. My husband and kids are settled here in Atlanta, so I don't have a chance."

6. *Physical condition*: It may not be politically correct to say so, but I must be honest with you: You *can't* do anything if you try hard enough. Some dreams *are* contingent on your physical ability. You can work out obsessively, practice religiously, and still not make it in the NBA if you're five-foot, seven-inches tall. There are ways to overcome this kind of hurdle, but they involve going back and refining the dream, not upping your exercise or going on a low-carbohydrate diet. I'll get into that later, but for now I'll just note that physical condition isn't always an insur-mountable obstacle caused by an irrational dream. In fact, for most people this worry is rational and realistic. For instance, the twenty-four-year-old young woman who told me, "No airline is going to hire someone who is as over-weight as I am to be a flight attendant."

7. *Education and training*: Just as physical condition may be a requirement for some dreams, so a specific education or training may be a *sine qua non* to succeed at certain Second Acts. You can no more become a massage therapist with-out getting the proper training, than you could practice as a physician without going to medical school. The lack of required education or training is an obvious barrier. Sometimes, it's not a total lack of training, but a question of degree. One forty-three-year-old depressed stockbroker who wanted to become a carpenter explained to me, "For a hobbyist, I'm a good furniture maker. But I just don't have the training to do this for a living."

8. *Timing*: It's very common to feel the timing just isn't right to launch a Second Act. Some explain they need to wait

until their lives or circumstances have changed in some way. Frequently, they say, "Now's not the time. Once my youngest finishes college in another five years I'll be able to start painting again. But until then I just need to stick it out." Others believe there's but a limited window of opportunity to pursue the life of their dreams . . . and that window is now shut. I hear that a lot from people whose dream involves parenthood. They say things like, "It's too late. The time to have a child would have been right after we got married, before our careers were set, and our lives became so complex and costly."

9. *Esteem*: It's incredible how much power over our lives we unconsciously give to other people. Even the most out-wardly secure and self-possessed individual often feels a conscious or subconscious need to win the approval of others, whether parent, peer, or someone else. We all worry far more about what others think of us than we often care to admit. That's why esteem is often an obstacle to changing your life. It's not often such hurdles are cited in conversation. Despite my readiness to admit much of what I did in my early life was to please my parents, peo-ple hate to admit how much they, too, care about what others think of them. Still, I do sometimes hear statements like these, "Everyone is going to think I'm crazy—a sixty-three-year-old grandma trying to become a dancer;" "My parents will simply not understand my wanting to adopt a child when I'm not even married."

10. *Fear of failure*: A lack of self-esteem is an obvious barrier to launching a Second Act. Of course, it's rarely framed that way to others. Instead, it's presented as the "realiza-tion" they simply don't possess the required elements it takes to pursue their dreams. Afraid they're not good

enough, for instance, to become a professional comedian, people say it's not worth even trying. "I know I'll never make it. I just don't have what it takes to become a comic. I'm not funny enough. So why put myself through the pain of failure?"

11. *Fear of success*: Ironically, many of the people whose fear of failure is an obstacle to their launching a Second Act, also have a fear of success that blocks their path to happiness. They'll say, even if by "some fluke" they achieve their dream, it won't last long. It will be taken away from them. In their eyes, every success has to eventually become a failure. And achieving a goal, only to lose it later would, they feel, be worse than never having achieved it all. So, they rationalize, it's better not to even go after the life of their dreams. I remember one thirty-nine-year-old woman who wanted to shift from being a magazine writer to a novelist saying to me, "Even if I do write a novel, and get someone to buy it, it will be a flop, and I'll never be able to sell another one. I don't want to face that kind of reversal. I'd rather not even try."

12. *Fatalism*: Finally, there are people whose pessimistic view of themselves or the world is an obstacle to their Second Act. They don't feel entitled to live the life of their dreams. They're fatalists; they believe they've been dealt a hand they can't change. Destiny is fixed, in their eyes, and they aren't going to have any more than they currently have or be any happier than they are right now. Of course, they think they could get more miserable. For instance, such people often feel launching a Second Act that's doomed to fail will make them feel even worse. I've found this fatalism obstacle often expressed in, what I call, the "bag lady fear:" "What's the point? I'm doomed to end up old and

---

Famous Second Act

BRIGITTE BARDOT

Camille Javal, ballet student and model from Paris, appeared on the cover of *Elle* in 1951 and one year later had her screen debut in Jean Boyer's *Crazy for Love*. Taking the name Brigitte Bardot, her performance four years later in the film *And God Created Woman*, made her an international star. Her surly sexuality led to her being called a "sex kitten." In 1973 the sex kitten started her Second Act, giving up her film career and devoting herself to campaigning for animal rights. ■

---

alone, dying in some shabby little apartment surrounded by nothing but the debris of an empty life." I've even heard this problematic feeling disguised as some kind of altruistic attitude, "Why should I get to do what I want when there are people who don't, or can't?"

FIVE EXERCISES TO REVEAL YOUR OWN CLOSED DOORS

I'm sure at least some of these dozen barriers resonate with you, whether you're feeling empowered or nervous. I realize they may not fit you exactly, but I hope they serve to start you thinking about the shut doors blocking you from living the life of your dreams. With these general hurdles in mind, let's get started on compiling your own list. To do that, I'd like to take you through four exercises.

The first two exercises have you focus on your past. The third asks you to concentrate on the present day, your current life. The fourth exercise requires you to become a bit of a seer and look into the future. If you recall, in Chapter 2 I said there was no requirement to do all of those exercises. Here, however, you really do need to do each of the exercises. Don't worry; none are debilitating or time consuming. You'll probably be able to go through all four on a weekend afternoon. And just as earlier, I strongly suggest you hold onto all the physical notes you make in this part of the process. They'll be invaluable when it comes to compiling your Second Act script. Now, take out your Second Act notebook, and let's start the first exercise.

Exercise 1

If you've now decided to pursue a long-held but suppressed dream, it's safe to assume there were reasons why you didn't go after this goal in the past. What were they? Perhaps you initially planned on having a big family. Maybe you dreamed of moving to a cabin in the Adirondacks.

Look back and try to remember the obstacles you that kept you from going after your goal. Perhaps you didn't have the self-confidence to enter a highly competitive field. It could be no one encouraged your dream and, as a result, you felt discouraged. Maybe you felt pressured to address immediate financial or familial needs. Were attitudes different then? Write the list in your notebook on a page titled PAST BARRIERS.

Try not to self censor. I'm not there to look over your shoulder and read what you wrote. And, there's no need to show your list to anyone else. If you didn't pursue a career in library science because, at the time, you thought it would hurt your chances to score with girls, or if you didn't pursue a career as a phys.-ed.

teacher because you were afraid people would think you were a lesbian, no one else is going to know about it.

Also, don't second guess yourself. Hindsight is 20/20. It's easy to see past mistakes. It's much harder to see them when you're in the heat of the moment. Besides, making mistakes is how we learn. You were a different person back then. You can have regrets, but remember your past mistakes as well as your former smart choices all went into making you the incomparable, incredible person you are today.

Include as much detail as you possibly can about each of those past barriers. If, for example, you didn't move to Seattle in the 1980s because you were afraid what your family and friends would say, note all you can remember about what you thought would be their criticisms. For instance, note what you imagined your mother saying about being so far from relatives, and what you pictured your best friend saying about you being flighty. Don't obsess over the accuracy of your memories. Perceptions and feelings are fine.

Barry Recalls the Closed Doors That Blocked Him in the Past

If you recall from Chapter 2, Barry D'Angelo is the owner of a bus leasing business inherited from his father. He is married and has two children. He had given up on the two pub-style restaurants he had opened on his own since the bus business offered a better income and more time with his family. An outgoing sort, Barry began exploring a Second Act after the funeral of an uncle who, despite family disapproval, had pursued his calling: a career in art and art education.

Barry had enjoyed the restaurant business, not because of his love of cooking, but because it was a safe and lucrative way for him to be the center of attention: to be on stage performing. The bus business simply didn't provide him with the thrill he needed.

Famous Second Act

JAMES CARVILLE

The oldest of eight children, James Carville was born in 1944 and grew up in a one stop sign Louisiana town named after his grandfather. His mother, Lucille, known to all as Miss Nippy, sold *World Book* encyclopedias door-to-door to put all her children through college. Carville left college to join the Marine Corps, served for two years, and then returned to Louisiana State for both his undergraduate and law degrees. Unhappy with his legal career, Carville spent much of his free time as a consultant and advisor to Democrats running for local- and state-wide offices. In 1989, at the age of forty-five, he launched his Second Act and teamed with Paul Begala to form the political consulting firm of Carville & Begala. The duo managed Bill Clinton's successful presidential campaign in 1992. Carville's Second Act went global in 1997 when he formed the international consulting firm Gold Greenberg Carville NOP. ■

After a great deal of soul searching and thought, and more than two months of working at defining and then distilling his dream, Barry came to realize he didn't want to go back into restaurants, he wanted to become an actor. He wanted, quite literally, a Second Act. At that point, I had Barry start going through the same exercises I'm outlining in this chapter.

Looking back, Barry tried to figure out why he hadn't pursued an acting career. It wasn't for a lack of self-confidence. Barry always loved to perform and entertain. Some of his earliest memories were of "entertaining" friends of his parents at dinner parties. As a five or six year old he'd do impressions for guests and act out his favorite scenes from movies or television. But somewhere along the line he decided not to pursue what he now believed was his calling. Upon reflection he realized it largely had to do with his family's beliefs about work and security. Both his parents were from poor families and had very strong work ethics and needs for financial security. Making money and having a secure income were the most important things in the world to Barry's father and mother. Acting just wasn't the kind of profession they'd understand. In college Barry studied business—the only nonprofessional field his folks thought worthy of the expense of a college education—and contented himself with doing stand-up comedy at local clubs and acting in a couple of student productions. Consent was definitely one of the barriers that in the past blocked Barry's pursuit of his dream.

But there was more to it than just that. Thanks to his father's drive and savvy, Barry grew up in an upper middle class environment. He never wanted for anything. His parents, having been brought up with nothing, saw possessions as a sign of success. Having a new bike, a stereo, stylish clothes, a new car, were all parts of Barry's youth. He knew an acting career, while potentially lucrative, would require lots of material sacrifice. To be honest, he didn't want to give up luxuries. When he graduated college he briefly flirted with the idea of moving into Manhattan with a couple of friends and trying to break into either comedy or the theater. However, he looked much harder for conventional employment. When he was offered a job as an assistant manager of a catering hall at a salary large enough for him to get his own apartment and buy a new car, he grabbed it. So money was also a barrier in the past, albeit in the unusual sense of his having had too much rather than not enough.

Okay, now it's time to get your head out of the past and to stop dwelling on regrets and failings. Set your Second Act notebook aside and make yourself a cup of coffee or tea. Grab a snack, too, if you'd like. When your tea is steeped or your coffee brewed, take up your notebook again.

Exercise 2

With a few minutes mental distance, and probably years of physical distance from facing those closed doors of the past, consider them in light of your current life. What has changed? Look over the list you recorded. Are any of the barriers that kept you from pursuing your dream in years past still blocking your way? Maybe you didn't pursue a singing career because the income wasn't enough to support a growing family, but today your children are grown and independent, your spouse is working, and your mortgage is paid off. Perhaps a very traditional parent who never would have supported a different life path, such as a move to another part of the country for an improved lifestyle, has become more open minded, or, unfortunately, passed on. It's even possible your physical condition has improved, making what once unlikely, say, being a mother, now very doable.

Turn to the list you compiled in the first exercise and cross off all those doors that are no longer closed. Once again, include as many details as you can without obsessively digging through your files. For example, you might note you used to have expenses of $3,000 a month but today, living in a smaller, fully paid up condo in a less expensive state, they've dropped to $2,000. Estimates are fine.

Do your best to be honest with yourself and about others. If, say, you're still worried how your spouse would react, don't falsely ascribe greater independence to yourself or tolerance to him. You'll only bump your head later if you now pretend a door is now open when it's still closed. Don't worry. I can help you open it—as long as you acknowledge it's there.

Please don't get angry with yourself if you only now discover all the obstacles that kept you from the life of your dreams are gone. Believe me, you haven't lost or wasted time. You've come to this realization at just the right moment. As I've said earlier: You're just where you should be.

Similarly, don't get frustrated because those same doors are still closed, continuing to block your path to happiness. In the second part of this book, you'll pick up the tools and techniques to knock them down once and for all.

Turn to a fresh page in your Second Act notebook and head it, CLOSED DOORS. Rewrite any barriers from the past you haven't crossed off the earlier list onto this page. Go to the list of twelve general obstacles that I presented earlier in this chapter and see which of them each of the barriers from your past most resembles. Add that information to the page simply by making a parenthetical note next to each item on the list.

Barry Determines How Things Have Changed.

Barry considered the two past barriers he had uncovered: parental consent and money. His father had died years ago, and while his influence remained, particularly in Barry's management of the bus leasing business, Barry no longer felt he needed his dad's approval. His mother had mellowed considerably over the intervening years, her ambitions for Barry satiated by his business and personal successes. Barry felt parental consent, or their influence, was no longer an issue. Similarly, money seemed to be a moot question now. . . at least in the way it was in years past. Barry and his wife, Maria, took his parents' materialism to the next level. While his parents drove Lincoln Continentals, he and Maria drove Mercedes. His parents had someone come in to help with the kids once a week. Barry and Maria had live-in help. He really felt his materialism was satisfied. He had all the creature comforts and toys he ever wanted, and he still wasn't happy. So, his need for the luxuries only money could buy was no longer an issue. But that didn't mean money, and perhaps even consent, weren't still closed doors in slightly different ways.

Exercise 3

Having reviewed what stopped you from pursuing your dream in the past, and noting which, if any, of those obstacles still remain, it's time to turn to the present. What barriers stand between you and your dream life today? Perhaps you don't feel able to start your own business because your financial obligations to your children have been replaced by financial obligations to aging parents. Maybe the years that have gone by make your age an issue in having a family. It could be the understandable desire to acquire the trappings of a "grown up life," has passed, only to lead to an increased appreciation for comfort and security. That could make going back to college daunting.

Give yourself some time to think through what would or could happen if you launched your Second Act right now. What problems could keep you from starting or could crop up along the way? Play out the whole scenario in your head. Your family members are at different stages in their lives today than in the past. How would they react now? Consider the impact on your income, savings, and expenses. You may have more today, but that could also mean you've more to lose. Roots are set, so relocation may now be an issue. Perhaps the time it would take to shift gears presents a new problem due to your current family or household dynamics.

Go back to the list of the twelve general barriers I outlined earlier and see which if any of them apply to your current life and the immediate pursuit of your dream. Be honest and open, but at the same time try not to manufacture nonexistent problems. The goal here isn't to come up with the most closed doors, it's to come with an accurate list of hurdles in your path. If you go through all these exercises and find there's nothing standing in your way, that's wonderful. You can just toss this book aside and get on with your Second Act. Believe me, my feelings won't be hurt. Maybe it took my pulling the scales from your eyes for you to see the truth. At the same time, don't fall victim to denial. Pretending a door is open when it's still closed won't make it go away.

Add whatever current barriers you've uncovered onto the list on the page in your notebook you've titled CLOSED DOORS. Determine which of the twelve general obstacles your own specific hurdles most resemble and make a note of your findings.

Barry Looks for New Closed Doors.

Barry's excitement at finding that the closed doors of his past no longer blocked his path vanished once he started looking for new barriers. At forty-three, he felt it was awfully late to get started in a competitive field like acting, so age was a problem. In addition, it could take years to establish himself as an actor, if ever. That meant duration was an issue.

Barry knew his wife and children would support his doing whatever made him happy; they had always made that clear. Even though he was now willing to trade material comforts for his dream he didn't want to force his family to sacrifice for him. Maria was a stay-at-home mom. The girls were able to pursue all their interests, both after school and in the summer. He didn't want that to change. So money was back on the list as an issue.

Finally, Barry's self-confidence was tempered by knowing he hadn't acted since college. While he felt he had raw talent, he was afraid he didn't have all the formal training he would need to make it as an actor.

At this point you can go and get yourself some lunch and relax for an hour or so. I want you to clear your head because the next exercise requires you to engage in some dire forecasting.

Exercise 4

I need you to briefly put aside the positive attitude you adopted after reading the previous chapter. Don't worry; this exercise will conclude with you feeling even more optimistic than before. But first, turn to a fresh page in your Second Act notebook and give voice to the fears that keep you awake at night. Call the page NIGHTMARES. Write down what could happen in the future to keep you from living the life of your dreams.

Go ahead; play out all those worst-case scenarios you've imagined, like the death of a parent or the destruction of your house in an earthquake. Express the secret insecurities you may never share, such as a spouse leaving you or your company going bankrupt. It doesn't matter whether the fear is likely to happen or a one in a million chance, potentially earth shattering, or possibly just a minor speed bump. What matters is you express these worries and get them down on paper.

Now, try to see what's underlying each of these nightmare scenarios. I don't mean you need to dig for the emotional or psychological reasons for the fears. Obviously that's something you could talk to a therapist about if you wanted. It's laudable, but for the purposes of launching your Second Act it's not necessary. I'm actually asking you to look for the concrete problem or obstacle each of these fears could present. Once again, go back to those twelve general barriers for a guideline.

For instance, why do you see the future death of a parent as a potential barrier to your Second Act? Believe me, I know it's a terrible thing to lose a parent. But what tangible impact would it have on your Second Act? It could be you're relying on them for financial backing. That would make it a possible money obstacle. Perhaps you're looking to them for encouragement and emotional support. In that case it's a potential esteem hurdle.

Once you've determined the underlying concrete problem for each future barrier, add it to the list on your CLOSED DOORS page. Make a note next to each indicating the general barrier you've found it reflects.

Barry Thinks of What Closed Doors He Could Face in the Future

Barry thought about what could crop up in the future to block his Second Act. Most of the worst-case scenarios and nightmares he conjured up didn't seem to have a direct impact on his acting dream. But, there was one that did seem a potential roadblock. He was afraid if his pursuit of acting success dragged on Maria would begin to resent him. While she was completely supportive today, he feared that might change if, for example, circumstances forced her to get a job. She had given up her teaching career when Barry opened his first restaurant. They both thought it important she stay home with the girls since his work would keep him out of the house just when they were home from school. Would she eventually grow resentful at having to sacrifice for him once again? He added consent to his list of closed doors.

Feeling a bit overwhelmed and depressed? It's understandable. In this chapter, I've had you dwell on negative feelings and fears about your future. In effect you've outlined all the ways your dream life could turn into a nightmare. If that's not a downer, I don't know what is. But here's the catch. You can get right back to that empowered optimistic attitude you developed in the previous chapter. How? By realizing every one of those past, present, and future obstacles, no matter how dire or dramatic, however monumental or earth shattering, can be overcome.

That's right. You can get over, through, under, or around each and every one. You can open every one of those closed doors. I'm here to tell you there's no obstacle that can't be overcome. In subsequent chapters, I'll be showing you how. But for now think about this: You've just given expression to every possible obstacle that could keep you from the living the life of your dreams, from the past to the future, from the realistic to the far fetched, and you've been told none of them are insurmountable. The worst possible circumstances you can imagine can't derail your Second Act. I can't think of anything more empowering than knowing that.

Take the rest of the day off and treat yourself. Do something you enjoy, and do something for someone else too, if you can. Take someone you love to dinner or a movie. Play with your children. Take your dog for a walk. Let yourself be happy.

Exercise 5

After letting your list of closed doors sit for a day or so, pick it up again. Now that you're back to feeling empowered, it's time to do one more exercise before we can start figuring out ways to break down those closed doors standing between you and the life of your dreams. We need to categorize the barriers you face as being either internal or external. That's because the two types of barriers are sometimes dealt with in different ways.

Internal barriers are obstacles inside your own head. They're self-generated fears, inhibitions, and attitudes.

External barriers are hurdles present in the real world. They're tangible, often physical, difficulties that could keep you from your dreams.

Don't just reflexively categorize your personal barriers. Spend the time to really go over your list with some care. You see, it's not always easy to tell which category a particular problem falls into until you've had a chance to analyze it.

For example, if age is a barrier to your changing careers, is it because you think you're too old to do something, or you've actually been told you're too old, say, by a perspective employer? If someone else whose approval you might need says you're too old, then your age is an external barrier. If you just think it's a problem, it's an internal barrier. Let's say you want to have a child. If your physician has run tests and discovered your chances of conceiving are low, or you've met with an adoption agency representative who has expressed concern with your age, you're facing an external barrier. But maybe you're just afraid you'll get those responses without actually soliciting them. In that case, it's an internal barrier.

You may have listed money as a closed door because you've made the calculations and have actually determined you can't cut your expenses sufficiently to live on a teacher's salary. But perhaps you've listed it because you've just assumed your family can't cope with a 40 percent cut in your income. If you've done the math, spoken with your family, and you just can't make the numbers work, then money is an external barrier. If you haven't done the work or are just expressing the feeling you don't want to give up dining out to live the life of your dreams, then money is an internal barrier.

Perhaps you believe it will take too long to launch your Second Act because you've researched all the options and found there's no way around, let's say, going to college full time for two years to get your MBA. Then again, you may have added it to your list because you've just let the possible sacrifices needed or the potential short cuts scare you off, or you haven't even checked whether there are alternatives. In the first case it's an external barrier; in the latter three cases it's internal.

If you're worried about another's consent or assistance, and you actually need their agreement or help to be able to launch your Second Act, then it's an external barrier. If you'll need someone else's approval strictly for emotional or psychological reasons, then getting it is an internal barrier. For example, if you'd like to have your parents' approval for your shift from stockbroker to pastry chef because you've always craved their approval, you're facing an internal barrier. On the other hand, if you need to borrow money from them to go to cooking school, their approval is an external barrier.

If location is truly vital to your Second Act—say your dream revolves around a specific locale—and you're unable to easily move, then you're facing an external barrier. If a change in location isn't really vital—just perhaps an advantage—or if you're unwilling rather than unable to move, it's an internal barrier. So, it's an external closed door if you want to be a professional tuna fisherman but you can't move from Phoenix. It's an internal closed door if you just don't want to move from Arizona.

Is physical condition truly a requirement for your Second Act? If so, and you really aren't physically capable of meeting those requirements, then you're facing an external barrier. On the other hand, if you're just assuming physical condition is a requirement, or you're afraid you won't physically measure up to a perceived rather than actual requirement, you're dealing with an internal barrier. Feel you can't be a model because you're five foot seven inches or an airline steward because you're 30 pounds overweight? Those are internal barriers until you find out for certain.

If your dream specifically requires you to have a certain educational or skill credential that you currently lack, then it is an external barrier. But if there's no mandate for the credential, and you simply believe it's needed, you're facing an internal barrier. Having a degree in journalism isn't a requirement to becoming a newspaper reporter, for instance, despite what many people think.

I don't think timing can ever be an external barrier. Second Acts by their very nature demonstrate there isn't just one window of opportunity to achieve your dreams. I believe life is a constant window of opportunity. By now you should realize every day is another chance to lead the life you want. If you're still viewing timing as a closed door, you're facing an internal barrier.

The same is true for fear of failure, fear of success, and fatalism. All those are symptoms of internal barriers—doors being slammed shut inside your head by your negative self image.

Similarly, I don't believe esteem is ever actually an external barrier. It's human nature to want people to like and respect you. It's comforting and reassuring to have others agree with the choices you make. If your best friend thinks you're doing the right thing, then you feel with some certainty you probably are. But it's also true if you let the opinions or feelings of others keep you from living the life of your dreams, you're doomed to unhappiness.

Whenever a client of mine repeatedly expresses concerns with timing and what others think, I like to quote the famous Jewish scholar Hillel,[9] "If I am not for myself, who is for me? If I am only for myself, what am I? And if not now, when?"

If after analyzing your own list of closed doors you're still not sure whether one is an internal or external barrier, ask yourself if the problem is in your control. It is, if you, on your own, can resolve or solve it. Alternatively, is the problem out of your control? That means you need someone or something else to change in order to surmount this hurdle. If you are in control of

---

[9] Hillel lived from around 30 BCE to 10 AD. He is regarded as the spiritual father of the collection of teachers who led the Jews of Palestine until 400 AD. He and another scholar named Shammai formed the most famous of the rabbinic *zuggot* (oppositional pairs) who debated philosophical and religious issues. Hillel usually took the more liberal stance. His most famous maxim is known as the golden rule. When asked to sum up the entire Torah in one sentence he is supposed to have said, "Do not unto others that which is hateful unto thee. All the rest is commentary."

it, it's an internal barrier. If you're not in control of it, it's an external barrier.

Once you go over all the closed doors on your list, make a note of whether each is an internal or external barrier to your living the life of your dreams.

Barry Categorizes His Closed Doors as Internal or External

Looking over his list of closed doors, Barry began noting which were internal and which were external barriers. When I met with him subsequently I saw the dispassionate approach he brought to business enabled him to do an excellent job of this on his own.

He realized his age was actually an internal barrier. There were actors of every age, and no one had actually told him he was too old to start acting.

His money fear was, on the other hand, an external barrier. While he and Maria had retirement savings and money put away for the kids' college tuition, giving up his business and income would have a huge impact. He calculated the family would, by sacrificing, be able to make their savings last for two years. But that would mean gambling all their futures on his dream.

Barry's concern about how long it would take to become a working actor was also an external barrier. Through the restaurant business he knew some very talented people who had spent years waiting on tables while waiting for their big break. . . which in some cases never came.

While there was no doubt further education and training could help Barry make it as an actor, they weren't really a requirement. Unschooled, untrained actors can get parts. It's rare, but it does happen. Barry listed training as an internal barrier.

Finally, because Maria had never expressed the slightest hint or hesitation about not backing him 100 percent, he decided his fear about her potential future resentment was an internal barrier.

Okay, you can now put your Second Act notebook away for a couple of days and go about your current life, content in the notion you're about to plan ways to break down all the closed doors keeping you from your dreams.

RANK YOUR CLOSED DOORS FROM HARDEST TO EASIEST TO KNOCK DOWN

After a couple of days away from your list of closed doors you'll be able to look at them with a fresher eye. Try to separate the closed doors into three categories: those so flimsy you are pretty confident they can be knocked down with a little effort; those so solid you're not sure you can knock them down; and those built of oak and lined with iron so you're convinced you'll never be able to get through them. My suggestion is you put "X" next to the first category, "XX" the second, and "XXX" next to the ones you think impossible to overcome. Now, look at those you've marked "XXX." Which is the one you least relish tackling; the one you're convinced will be the single biggest obstacle to your Second Act; the toughest closed door to knock down? That's the one you should tackle first.

I know some people believe you should start small so you develop momentum when faced with a set of challenges. But in this case I don't think it's necessary. You see, I want you to be as confident as I am you can overcome every obstacle you face. I want you to go after the closed door you think the most difficult to break down, because after you realize you can get through it successfully, the rest will be easy to crack. I want you to be as happy and excited and upbeat and empowered as possible, as soon as possible.

Still don't believe me? Well, look at it this way: If you read about your most difficult task first, and don't accept my strategies and tactics will work, you can toss this book away with the minimum time investment. You'll be free to go back to your currently unsatisfying life that much sooner.

So, turn next to the chapter in Part 2 of the book that deals with your most daunting closed door. Once you read all the chapters dealing with the barriers you're facing, you can turn to Chapter 13, which explains how to create the script for your Second Act. By the time you get there, your Second Act, the life of your dreams, will be in sight.

OPENING THE DOORS TO YOUR SECOND ACT

"It is not because things are difficult that we do not dare; it is because we do not dare that they are difficult."

—SENECA

CHAPTER 5

Age:
Perception versus Reality

"To admire, to expand one's self, to forget the rut, to have a sense of
newness and life and hope, is to feel young at any time of life."
—CHARLES HORTON COOLEY

You're never too old or too young to do something. Age obstacles are always due to the misperception that age is somehow
indicative of physical condition, mental acuity, wisdom, maturity,
or some other necessary trait. In fact, I believe the only thing that
can now safely be assumed by a birth date is how many candles
should go on a birthday cake. Age is a meaningless factor.

I know: Saying that is the easy part. . . especially for someone
who got his bachelors degree at fifty-eight and became a partner
at a new law firm at age sixty-nine. Getting *you* to believe it, and
giving you the tools to get *others* to believe it will require a bit
more work.

Let me make it clear, even though I'm currently seventy-three,
I'm not just advocating the rights of older people. While I believe
I'm living proof you're never too old to accomplish your goals, I
also believe you're never too young. After all, I graduated from
law school at age twenty. And while I know I'm good at what I

do, when it comes to accomplishments at early and advanced ages, I'm not unique.

It's also important for you to realize you've got the law and most of the business world on your side as well. A bank, for example, doesn't care about your age when you apply for a loan. As long as you're over eighteen, and are, therefore, legally responsible, it will write you loan if you can demonstrate the willingness and ability to pay it back. A bank will make a million dollar loan to a nineteen year old or give a thirty-year mortgage to an eighty year old. Age just doesn't matter.

If you believe, however, without any direct evidence, others are going to think you're too old or too young to pursue your chosen Second Act, then age is an internal barrier for you. The first two exercises in this chapter will help you re-examine your own attitudes toward age. The third exercise will demonstrate that the factors you associate with age can be advantages rather than disadvantages. Finally, the fourth exercise will show there are others who've pursued similar paths without letting age stop them. (One quick note: If you believe you're too old to launch your Second Act, start with the first exercise; if you believe you're too young, start with the second.)

If age is an external, rather than internal barrier for you, I still encourage you to do the earlier exercises in this chapter. They'll be a big help in boosting your spirits and providing a solid foundation for the subsequent exercises and efforts. However, you'll find the nuts and bolts techniques for overcoming others external age barriers toward the end of the chapter.

THERE'S NO SUCH THING AS BEING TOO OLD.

Why do you think you're going to be labeled as being too old? Probably, it's because you've a very traditional attitude toward age. Let's set aside your assumptions and look at the facts.

Society has taken to labeling someone who reaches age sixty-five as being old. Why? Likely because that's the age originally established for Social Security eligibility by the Roosevelt administration back in the 1930s. They took that age from Bismarck, Chancellor of Germany, who a century earlier decided that was the age civil servants in his newly unified Germany could collect their pensions. The New Dealers were being economical. At the time they proposed sixty-five was old, life expectancy was about sixty-two. But today, average American life expectancy is about seventy-seven. If you just consider white females, it's up to eighty. At the beginning of the twentieth century the average adult life span was from about age twenty to age fifty. Today, adult life runs from twenty to eighty. You've now got thirty more years of adulthood; twice the amount of time your grandparents had. Those additional years just cry out to be filled with a Second Act.

Make no mistake. We're not talking about thirty added years of decrepitude either. New attitudes and approaches to medicine, nutrition, and exercise aren't just adding years of existence to our life spans, they're adding years of fully active living. As longevity researcher Lydia Bronte[10] has noted, while longevity has increased, the aging process has slowed, resulting in all those extra years being added to a productive middle age, not a feeble old age.

Just think about your own life and those around you, and you'll be able to see the changes in activity level.

Exercise 1

Take out your Second Act notebook and turn to a fresh page. Divide it into four columns vertically. Label the second column ME, the third PARENTS, and the fourth GRANDPARENTS. Go

---

[10] Author of *The Longevity Factor*

Famous Second Act

RONALD REAGAN

When a Hollywood agent signed him to a film contract in 1937, Midwestern radio sportscaster Ronald Reagan began one of America's most remarkable lives. As a contract player with Warner Brothers Studio, Reagan appeared in more than fifty feature films. During World War II he made training films for the Air Force. After the war Reagan worked as spokesman for General Electric and then as host of the television series "Death Valley Days." Long active in union politics, Reagan's Second Act began when he shifted his affiliation from Democrat to Republican and became an active promoter of 1964 presidential candidate Barry Goldwater. Two years later he was elected governor of California. He served two terms, during which he campaigned for the Republican presidential nomination as the standard bearer of the party's conservative wing. In 1980 he finally won the Republican nomination on his third try and then defeated incumbent Jimmy Carter. Four years later he won re-election. ■

---

to the first column and, just below the line where you've written the other labels, write the number 20. Skip down about five lines and write 30. Keep skipping the same number of lines, and write 40, 50, 60, 70, and 80.

Let's fill in your column first. What were you doing and what was your life like at the decade of your life indicated by the number in the far left column? Perhaps you were in graduate school in your twenties. Maybe your hobby was backpacking. You may have held a part-time job in addition to your schooling. It could be you had an active social life or were just setting up a household with your partner. In as few words as possible try to give a description of your life at that time that deals primarily with your physical activities, rather than attitudes and ideas. A good short cut is to think about what your daily, weekly, and monthly schedules were like. After you've finished examining your life in your twenties, do the same for as many subsequent decades as you've been alive.

With your column filled, turn to your parents column. Do your best to describe what your parents lives were like at those decades. Obviously, you're not going to have the same level of detail as in your own column, but be as thorough as possible. A good short cut for this is to view your parents lives through the prism of your own. Figure out what ages you were in the given decade and then think back to what your parents were doing in relation to you. Let's say you were ten when your mother and father were about thirty. Did your Mom drop you off at school every morning? Maybe she packed your lunch, and then had dinner on the table for when your father came home from work. Perhaps your father left early in the morning for a commute to his job and didn't come home until just before dinner. On weekends maybe he mowed the lawn while your mother cooked Sunday dinner. Just get down as much as you can, once again focusing on physical activities.

In the fourth column, try to do the same for your grandparents' lives. This will be the least detailed column, but that doesn't mean it won't provide some insights. If you can, think back to what your parents told you about their own childhood and early lives. Again, focus on what your grandparents physically did at different periods in their lives.

After you've finished filling in the page, start examining the chart. But this time, scan horizontally rather than vertically. What is your life like, say, in your forties, compared to what your parents and your grandparents lives were like in their forties? Look at all the ranges and see what jumps out at you. I'll bet, starting in the thirties, your life has been more active and energetic and complex than your parents' lives, and your parents' lives were more active and energetic than your grandparents' lives. And I'll also bet that trend continues for each subsequent decade.

Let's say you're a sixty-five-year-old retiree. Think back to your grandmother at age sixty-five. Can you picture her walking lap after lap around her community or playing golf or tennis as you might be doing? Maybe you're a forty-five year old whose kids are just leaving the nest. Compare yourself to your parents at that age. Could you imagine them going to see their equivalent of a Bruce Springsteen concert, or taking a canoeing trip through the Adirondacks?

Ironically, while psychologically and emotionally society hasn't completely absorbed and accepted that age isn't a factor in performance, the law has required it be ignored. The Age discrimination in Employment Act of 1967 (ADEA) made it unlawful to discriminate against a person, forty years or older, because of his or her age, with respect to any term, condition, or privilege of employment.[11] State laws all across the nation extend that protection to areas of life other than employment. Of course, just because it's illegal doesn't mean it doesn't happen. Later in this chapter, I'll show you how to keep age from ever being an issue.

---

[11] One important aside about the ADEA: It is generally unlawful for apprenticeship programs or internship programs to discriminate on the basis of an individual's age. For someone looking to embark on a new career path, an internship or apprenticeship can be an excellent way to get your feet wet. Companies are often eager for *older* interns or apprentices because it provides them with added value without added cost.

For now I simply want you to look over your chart again a few times and repeat to yourself, over and over, "you can't be too old to do anything."

THERE'S NO SUCH THING
AS BEING TOO YOUNG.

Are you afraid others are going to think you're too young? That's just as much a misperception as fearing you're too old. Young people are, by and large, far more mature, aware of their world, and active in their communities, at an earlier age than ever before.

Just as longevity has been increased due to better health and nutrition, so has physical maturity. Boys and girls have experienced puberty at younger ages than in previous generations. According to research, in North America the age of puberty has decreased by three to four months each decade after 1850. Obviously, I'm not suggesting a ten year old just entering puberty is the equivalent of an adult. Biological development isn't the same things as emotional maturity. But the statistics do show there's some kind of ongoing biological shift taking place.

Overlaying this biological shift are sociological changes that are creating more mature, aware, and active teens and young adults. David Elkind, an expert on childhood development,[12] has noted that changing family values have led children to grow up more quickly. The prototypical nuclear family of the 1940s and 1950s had certain core values. People believed and preached there was one perfect mate in the world for everyone and, having found each other, couples would live happily ever after with little or no

---

[12] Author of *The Hurried Child: Growing Up Too Fast Too Soon* and *All Grown Up and No Place to Go* among other works.

effort. In the 1940s and earlier it was common to believe women possessed a maternal instinct that meant they constantly wanted to be with their children. And, for the families of the 1950s, home and family were the centers of everyone's lives.

All of these notions have changed, creating young people today who are far more mature, aware, and active than pervious generations. Divorce has been commonplace for decades, making it clear to children that relationships don't always go on happily or last ever after. But remarriage has been more usual as well, demonstrating there isn't just one perfect match for every person. Relationships are no longer as bound by traditional gender roles. So while they may have become less romantic, they are more egalitarian, giving the children who grew up in the 1960s and later a more realistic view of relationships. To provide for the family, parents have, since the 1970s, needed to focus outside the home on their own work activities. That forced the children of those families to be more autonomous as well. The iconic "latch key child" learned to be independent and somewhat self sufficient at a younger age. All this autonomy led to a focus on the needs of the individual members of the family, rather than the needs of the family as a unit. That tendency continues to accelerate over the years. Today, a parent's meeting with a client or a child's dance recital is seen as being far more important than a family dinner together.

Other changes in our society forced young people to confront things of which they used to be ignorant. Exposure to information forced parents of the 1970s to explain difficult things to their children at earlier ages. Parents understandably needed to give their children the skills needed to successfully navigate in the world. But in the process they came face to face with things at earlier ages. Young people growing up in the 1970s and 1980s learned how to say no to drug dealers, just as young people growing up today learn how to ward off sexual predators. This awareness led to increased activism and involvement, whether in raising funds for the Boy Scout Troop's annual field trip, or holding a rally for Mothers Against Drunk Driving.

Need proof of how adult awareness has been coming earlier? Take a look at your own life and the lives of those around you.

Exercise 2

Take out your notebook and turn to a fresh page. Divide it into four columns vertically. Label the second column ME, the third PARENTS, and the fourth GRANDPARENTS. Go to the first column and, just below the line where you've written the other labels, write the number 20. Skip down about five lines and write 30. Keep skipping the same number of lines, and write 40, 50, 60, 70, and 80.

Let's fill in your column first. What were your attitudes about your life and what was your role in the community at the decade of your life indicated by the number in the far left column? Perhaps in your twenties you were a pacifist and were active in the antiwar protest movement. Maybe you were an internationalist and involved in the ROTC program at your university. You may have campaigned for a local congressperson you admired. After you've finished examining your life in your twenties, do the same for as many subsequent decades as you've been alive. It could be you took an active role in the PTA at you child's elementary school. Maybe you began volunteering at a local soup kitchen. In as few words as possible, try to give a description of your life during each decade that focuses primarily on your attitudes and ideals. A good short cut is to think about what social and political issues concerned you locally, nationally, and internationally. Another tip is to think about whether or not you had opinions about hot button issues such as women's rights, racial diversity, affirmative action, gay rights, and abortion.

With your column filled, turn to your parents column. Do your best to describe what your parents attitudes were like at those decades. Obviously, you're not going to have the same level as detail as in your own column, but be as thorough as possible. See whether you can recall their level of awareness and involvement. Did you argue with your parents about politics when your father was in his fifties? Maybe your mother started volunteering for the church in her sixties. See whether you can recall their having opinions about the hot button issues of the time.

Try to do the same for your grandparents lives in the fourth the column. This will be the least detailed column, but that doesn't mean it won't provide some insights. If you can, think back to the discussions or debates you heard your parents engage in with your grandparents. Again, focus on what your grandparents' attitudes, awareness, and involvement with the community were at different periods in their lives.

After you've finished filling in the page, start examining the chart. Scan it horizontally rather than vertically. What were your attitudes or activities like, say, in your thirties, compared to what your parents and your grandparents attitudes were like? Look at all the ranges and see what jumps out at you. I'll bet, starting in the twenties, you had far more opinions about far more issues than your parents and your grandparents, and you were far more active in your community. And I'll also bet that trend continues for each subsequent decade. What your opinions were or are, and what community activities you were or are involved with doesn't matter. What matters is you were aware and involved.

I'm not arguing maturing earlier has been either a positive or negative development. Good cases can be made for both. I'm just saying it has indeed taken place and you need to factor it into your view of yourself and the world. Even if you think it was generally an unfortunate development there was at least one positive aspect: Your youth should no longer be viewed as a handicap. As long as the law allows it, you can't be too young to do anything.

Unfortunately, the law hasn't expanded to protect young people as effectively as older adults. Nearly all age discrimination statutes apply only to those 40 years old and above. Not having legal leverage removes one, but not all, the tools you can use to overcome age obstacles.

NEGATIVE ASSOCIATIONS CAN ALSO BE POSITIVE.

Next, let's examine the factors you thought others would negatively associate with your age.

Exercise 3

Turn to a fresh page in your notebook, label it AGE WORRIES, and start listing all the age-related qualms you think others will have about your pursuing your chosen Second Act.

Are you afraid people will think you'll be resistant to change because you're fifty-two years old? Write that down. Maybe you're worried they'll think you won't have sufficient energy to work the long hours required by your chosen Second Act. Make a note of it. Similarly, if you believe people will think that because you're twenty-six, you won't have the seasoning to make tough choices, put that on your list. You might be concerned they think a young person doesn't have the perseverance necessary for success. If so, jot it down.

Go over the list of factors in your notebook and try to reduce the language to one word for each. For example, resistance to change could be described as obstinate or stubborn. A word for lacking perseverance could be peripatetic. Turn to a fresh page in your Second Act notebook. If you're worried you could be perceived as being too old, across the top of the page you should write OLD =.

If you're worried about being perceived as too young, write YOUNG = on top of the page. Next, list all the single word descriptions you came up with earlier. For instance: Old = obstinate, frail; Young = tentative, peripatetic.

I want to take you back to Chapter 2 for a moment. If you recall, one of the exercises I put you through was to ask your personal focus group about your traits and then try to come up with a reverse spin for each adjective. In other words, you took the positive traits or strengths offered and viewed them in a negative light, and took the weaknesses or negative traits noted and spun them positively. If someone said you were "pompous," for example, you spun it as "confident."

Now, take the single word descriptions you've listed that describe the negative statements or feelings you're afraid others will have or make about your age and spin them into positives. Being stubborn could be seen as being dogged or determined. Tentative? No, you're thoughtful. You're not inexperienced, you're fresh and open to new ideas. Weak? Of course not, you're cerebral. I will bet you a free one hour's telephone consultation you can't come up with an age-related fear that can't be spun positively.

To give you a hand with coming up with alternative spins for the most common stereotypes of old and young people, I've come up with the following little chart:

Stereotype	Positive Spin
plodding	careful
stubborn	determined
stale	seasoned
irresponsible	creative
flighty	energetic
inexperienced	open minded
impatient	ambitious
backward	experienced

Stereotype	Positive Spin
conventional	reliable
unreliable	unconventional
loner	entrepreneurial
meek	team player
expensive	valuable
negative	thoughtful
rash	innovative

Don't worry just yet about how to sell others on this reverse spin. That's not the purpose of the exercise. What matters now is that you realize and accept that there is indeed a positive spin for every negative you're projecting. As long as you're willing to accept that your age, whatever it is, can be a positive trait, it will be simple to convey that to others. Trust me.

YOU'RE NOT THE FIRST, AND YOU WON'T BE THE LAST.

I wasn't the first person to launch a Second Act, and you're not going to be the last. Throughout this book I've sprinkled stories of famous Second Acts. I could have included lots more. One of the most interesting threads that runs through all success stories is that age never plays a factor in any of them. Too young to start a business? Steve Jobs was twenty-one when he started Apple Computer. Of course, he had the help of his older friend Steve Wozniak . . . who was twenty-six. Too old to start a business? Harlan Sanders started Kentucky Fried Chicken at age seventy.

Exercise 4

Take a trip back to your local library and look for books, magazines, and articles that deal with the Second Act you're planning.

113

Famous Second Act

STEVE JOBS

Steve Jobs is the perfect example of someone whose Second Act brought him full circle. Adopted as an infant by a family in Northern California, Jobs attended Homestead High School in Cupertino. There he became friendly with Steve Wozniak. After briefly attending Reed College in Portland, Oregon, and then trekking through India, Jobs returned to California. There he reconnected with Wozniak who was working for Hewlett Packard and building computers to impress fellow members of the Homebrew Computer Club. Believing Wozniak's invention could attract more than just computer hobbyists, Jobs persuaded Wozniak to join with him and form Apple Computers

Give some thought to which of the popular magazines in your area of interest might have stories about people like you. For instance, if you're thinking of starting a business, look at magazines like *Inc.*, *Wired*, or *Fast Company* that focus on smaller and more recent firms, rather than *Fortune*, *Forbes,* and *Business Week* that tend to write about larger, more established companies. If you're planning on starting a family in your forties, look to publications like *Woman's Day*, *Ladies Home Journal*, and *Good Housekeeping*, which cater to women over thirty, rather than *Cosmo*, *Vogue,* or *Glamour,* which center on women in their twenties.

The reference librarian can also help you find indices, abstracts, and guides that will make the search easier, or steer you to the right electronic search tool. Just look for stories of those who've

in Jobs's garage in 1976. Jobs was twenty-one. Apple, in effect, created the personal computer market, and in the process, became a $335 million company. However, Apple began losing market share to competitors, primarily IBM. Although the revolutionary Macintosh introduced the graphical user interface and mouse to computing, it wasn't enough to keep Jobs from being ousted from the company in 1985. He went on to found NeXT Software and purchased Pixar Animation Studios. When Apple bought NeXT, Jobs was invited back to become interim CEO of Apple in 1996. Thus, began his Second Act. . . at the age of forty-one. After shepherding the introductions of the popular and successful iMac and iBook products, Jobs was appointed permanent CEO in 2000. ∎

---

succeeded in what you're attempting. I'll bet you find people both younger and older than you who succeeded.

Do some online research as well. Go to sites like biography. com, and type search terms that describe what you'd like to become. For example, key in "actor" or "musician." Scan through the results, and I guarantee you'll find examples of people who transcended age expectations and stereotypes, (By the way, you'll also find lots of people whose fame resulted from a Second Act.) When you find these examples, photocopy the articles or entries, or print out the Web pages and add them to your Second Act notebook. On top of each page write, "He/She did it, and so can I."

In all your subsequent readings and searches keep one eye peeled for other success stories. When you come across one, copy it and add it to your Second Act notebook. One can never have

---

Famous Second Act

Harlan Sanders

With only a sixth-grade education, Harlan Sanders thought he'd finally found his niche when, in 1929, at the age of thirty-nine, he opened a combination gas station/restaurant in Corbin, Kentucky. The business did well, particularly after 1939 when he started using a pressure cooker to make chicken very quickly. But then came World War II. His customer base started shrinking with people either moving north to factory jobs or joining the military. A new interstate opened after the war, eliminating his drive-by trade. By 1956, Sanders had to sell the business just to pay off his debts. After almost

---

too much inspiration. (Feel free to duplicate any of the stories of famous Second Acts I've included throughout this book and add them to your Second Act notebook as well.)

With your attitudes toward age no longer a barrier to your Second Act, it's time to explore ways to make sure others' attitudes toward age don't keep you from succeeding. You need techniques to get people to set aside their reflexive age prejudices long enough for you to demonstrate you possess the traits they think you'd lack due to your age. In effect, you need to ensure the first impression you make on someone doesn't trigger any age bias.

There are two types of first impressions: indirect and direct. Indirect first impressions are generated by things like your resumé, curriculum vitae, business plans, applications, written correspondence, email, telephone calls, or referrals from others, in which there is no physical contact. Direct first impressions are

thirty years in business, and at almost seventy, Harlan Sanders could have retired. He didn't. He choose to launch a Second Act. Sanders started demonstrating his pressure cooking technique and secret seasonings to other restaurant owners. In exchange for his secrets, they became Colonel Sanders franchises. In the first two years he only sold five franchises, but then sales started to take off. By 1960, he had sold 200. Four years later, at the age of seventy-four, having sold more than 600 franchises, he sold the franchising business, remaining on as spokesman. Sanders' incredible Second Act didn't end until his death in 1980 at the age of ninety. Today, the KFC chain has stores in more than eighty-two countries. ■

face-to-face meetings. I call the techniques for getting past bias in indirect first contacts age avoidance. The techniques for overcoming bias in direct first contacts I call age camouflage.

In outlining these techniques I'll be using examples from job searches. That's because I've found those are the most common situations when age is a prime obstacle. The same techniques can be adopted easily to fit other situations.

LEARNING AGE AVOIDANCE

It's wrong, morally and ethically, to discriminate against someone because of his or her age. It's also illegal to discriminate against someone, forty or older, because of his or her age. There's a big difference between determining someone can't do a job because he or she lacks the relevant experience or a certain physical ability, and assuming that, because of age, he or she automatically lacks that experience or physical ability. Unfortunately, not everyone will go through the prior three exercises and set aside unwarranted age bias.

In response, I think it's entirely justifiable to do everything possible to avoid disclosing or revealing your age during indirect first contacts. I believe it's the equivalent of doing your best to trim your tax bill, which is not only legal and ethical, but your patriotic duty. I don't think outright lying about your age is a legitimate technique. That's the same as tax evasion, which is illegal and unethical.

Practicing age avoidance will dramatically lower any age barriers you face in your Second Act. (Age camouflage will eliminate them all together.) That's because almost all indirect first contacts are used as negative screening devices. Let me explain. If someone is looking to, let's say, hire an assistant, they put a classified ad in the newspaper and ask interested parties to send a resumé and a cover letter with salary requirements. When they have a pile of responses they go through them, using the material to filter out candidates, not to choose someone to hire.

Indirect first contacts don't win you your goal, for instance, a job. They simply get you into the running, in this case, by getting you an interview. People use whatever information they gather indirectly as a means to disqualify you. If the first impression you make with the information you provide doesn't fit the template they have drawn up in their head for a successful candidate, however relevant that template may or may not be, you don't make the cut. Resumés, and any other indirect first impressions you make, don't get you jobs, or result in success. . . they get you interviews, or put you in position to succeed. The goal then, is to make sure the first indirect impression you make does nothing to disqualify you. In situations when you know your age will be an issue, that means doing everything you can to obscure your age.

Exercise 5

Gather up all the written information you've provided about yourself in the past. That includes resumés, bios, business plans, telephone scripts, talking points, and anything else you've used to initiate contact with people.[13] You're going to go through it all with a fine tooth comb.

Begin by directly eliminating all specific references to dates or ages. Say you earned a bachelor's degree from Ohio State in 1974 and note that on your resumé. Someone intent on using age as a screening technique would presume you graduated at the traditional age of about twenty-one, making you fifty today. Perhaps they'd feel that was too old for a candidate to fill the entry-level position in a field you're looking to shift to in your Second Act. Similarly, if your business plan states you graduated from New York University in 1999, a biased potential investor would infer you were twenty-five, and possibly think you were too young to be able to successfully start a business. Instead of providing a date, simply note or say you are a graduate of the university in question.

Go through any employment history listing you've created and remove dates as well. Not only would the starting date of your first listing give an indication to your age, but so would the length of time you held any one job. For instance, if the first job you list includes dates from 1995 to 1999 it would be easy for an

---

[13] By telephone scripts I'm referring to notes you prepare for your own use during telephone conversations. I'm a firm believer in scripting and having material prepared in advance so you're never at a loss for words. In this instance the script would contain ways you could offer the information verbally without giving any age hints. I use the phrase talking points to refer to a similar document I suggest people give to friends or intermediaries who will be approaching someone on their behalf.

age-conscious individual to infer you are about twenty-nine today. In written documents simply eliminate the information. If you're providing the information orally come up with phrasing that doesn't involve time frames, but instead focuses on your role. Examples include "I managed. . ."; "I supervised. . ."; and "I administered. . . ."

Similarly the number of jobs you list is a clue to your age. Provide too many listings, and you make it clear you've been in the job market for a long time. . . maybe too long for some people. Include too few, and they'll assume you're still wet behind the ears and don't have sufficient experience. The solution is to call your job listing "Employment Highlights" and to include only between three and five jobs without any dates. If you don't have enough relevant highlights divide jobs you've held into different listings based on changed titles or responsibilities. For example, if you were a salesperson at a retail operation and were promoted to assistant manager, list those as two separate highlights. To avoid the appearance you're trying to hide something, note, either at the end of any documents or during subsequent discussions, that you can provide a comprehensive employment history as well as references upon request.

Next, scour your listing of achievements.[14] The secret here is to, once again, focus on what's important without providing unsolicited hints about your age. You do this by providing the right kind of details. For example, noting you increased efficiency by reorganizing "the typing pool" is going to set off alarm bells about your advanced age. Alternatively, noting you personally

---

[14] I believe the primary element of all resumés should be a description of achievements or accomplishments rather than a chronological listing of jobs you've held. People are hired to get something done. And the best evidence they're capable is having accomplished the same thing in the past. The fact you've held similar jobs isn't proof you're capable of achieving what's required.

supervised the web site's shift from Flash to Quicktime 6 technology will lead some to think you're young. After all, they'd think, only a "kid" could be have hands-on knowledge about a recent technological development. The answer is to provide different details and use language that makes the achievement timeless. For example, reorganizing the typing pool could be described as "reorganized support staff resulting in 37 percent increase in efficiency." The shift in web technology could be phrased like this, "Administered adoption of next generation technology leading to 15 percent cut in costs." Describe all accomplishments by approximately how much you increased revenue, cut costs, or boosted efficiency, and you'll provide details to whet someone's appetite, while being able to leave out details that would let them figure out your age.

Personal details are often added to information packages as an afterthought, or in an effort to fill out a page. While not as important as other types of age avoidance, selecting the right details offers a chance to subtly use readers' biases to your advantage. Details such as race, religion, gender, and marital status should be avoided, because all they offer is an opportunity to discriminate without recourse. But listing your interests and hobbies provides a chance to send a message. If someone sees or hears an applicant is a fan of Gilbert and Sullivan, plays bridge competitively, and loves to sail, how will they picture the applicant? Stereotyping would lead them to assume it's a mature individual. Alternatively, how will they picture a person who says that they are a fan of Moby, play ice hockey, and love rock climbing? All those are stereotypically the interests of younger people. I would never suggest you make things up to create a false impression. But there's nothing wrong with selecting details to create the impression that gives you the best chance to make the cut. In general, physically dangerous pursuits and popular culture imply youth, while cerebral activities and classical culture imply maturity.

Similar stereotypes apply to the appearance of any documents. For instance, an information package done in a very stylized design, with modern graphics and colors, giving prominence to email addresses and URLs, would send the message the person who created it was youthful. Very traditional black and white documents, using standard serif typefaces and watermarked paper, giving priority to mailing addresses and telephone numbers, would be perceived as coming from a mature individual. Choose a design and style based on the message you want to convey.

I don't suggest you try to alter your voice in any way. Instead, concentrate on speaking clearly and being enthusiastic in tone. That conveys an ageless positive message.

LEARNING AGE CAMOUFLAGE

Your efforts at age avoidance will inevitably enable you to make an excellent indirect first impression. You'll soon have a face-to-face meeting of some kind lined up. That's when you'll need to shift from age avoidance to age camouflage.

If you recall, back in Chapter 3 I said your outsides always match your insides; if you believe you will succeed, you will project optimism to others and it will, in fact, help you succeed. The same is true for overcoming age obstacles. If you have truly accepted and internalized the lesson learned in the first three exercises of this chapter—that age is irrelevant—then you will project that and it will help convince others. Once you've had a chance for your confidence, determination, and skills to come through, your age won't matter.

But in order to guarantee you get that chance you'll need to amplify the message. That's because, in general, people make judgments, form opinions, and reach decisions, within the first three minutes of meeting someone for the first time. It sounds crazy, but those first impressions are vital. By and large a person spends the rest of a meeting with someone new finding reasons to rationalize the reaction they had in those first three minutes. If you clearly make your age irrelevant in those first three minutes, the natural confidence you'll project thereafter will provide all the backup and justification the other person needs. Win the first 180 seconds, and you achieve your goal. It's as simple as that. So how do you avoid age bias in those first three minutes? By packaging, or camouflaging, yourself.

By using the word camouflage I don't mean to imply you'll be disguising your age. Camouflage isn't always a total disguise. Some of the most effective camouflage serves to create a momentary hesitation in the other party.[15] That's what we're looking for. Let's be honest. Unless you have extensive plastic surgery, it will be fairly easy for the other person to at least guess your approximate age.[16] And, if they're brazen enough, they can get around age discrimination laws to try to fish out your age.[17] The secret is to change the sensory signals you send so the other person doesn't make a snap judgment.

If the bad news is you have only 180 seconds to win another party over, the good news is the easiest part of a meeting to seize control of are the first three minutes.

---

[15] In World War 2 naval vessels used what was called splinter camouflage. Rather than trying to make the ship disappear in the water, it created visual confusion in viewers as to its exact direction and speed.

[16] Don't get me wrong. I'm not opposed to plastic surgery. As you'll see in the chapter dealing with overcoming physical obstacles, I don't think there's anything wrong with having surgery to help you succeed at your Second Act.

[17] By law, an interviewer cannot ask how old you are, when you graduated high school or college, or what is your birth date. All they can legitimately ask is if you are over the age of 18.

Exercise 6

First, consider your garb. If you don't want to look old, avoid old-looking clothing. I'm not suggesting you try to dress like a young fashion model—a fifty year old with a pierced eyebrow will look ridiculous not youthful. You just need to dress stylishly. For a man that might mean a monochromatic shirt and tie; a four button, single-breasted suit; and slip-ons rather than wing tips. For a woman it could mean subtle makeup and no pearls, a knee-length skirt or pants rather than a standard business suit, and high heels.

Alternatively, if you don't want to look young, dress like a grown-up. Dress like you're on trial for your life. Your look should be conservative and traditional, not funky and cutting edge. For a man, that's perhaps a dark blue or gray three-button suit, with a white or light blue shirt, regimental stripe tie, and wing tips. For a woman maybe it's hair no longer than shoulder length and not short enough to be spiky, and a conservative business suit with simple shoes and pearls. In general, jewelry should be so subtle it's barely noticeable. The same for perfume or cologne. Patchouli oil won't lead anyone to think a thirty year old is just out of college. And Old Spice won't make a twenty-five year old seem like an experienced hand. Let your clothing, not your aroma do the talking.[18]

Next, make sure your mannerisms and body language deliver the right message. If you're worried about being thought of as too old, make sure to enter a room with energy and a bounce to your step. Smile with your eyes as well as your mouth; that will

---

[18] Speaking of aromas, no matter what age signal you're trying to send or camouflage, your breath and body odor must be inoffensive. Stop in a rest room to check, and pop a breath mint before a meeting, making sure to discretely spit it out before you enter.

instantly cut ten years off your age. Shake hands firmly and make direct eye contact. Convey enthusiasm but remain humble so you're not seen as a threat. Sit with your body back in your seat to show you're not stooped from age. Lean forward from the shoulders when the other party speaks to show animated interest. Never cross your legs or arms, it's perceived as being antagonistic. Always take a moment to think when responding to questions, during which you can lean back from the shoulders and look up. This shows you're taking the questions seriously and are giving them some thought. Don't look to the sides when the other person is speaking, that will imply boredom. Never interrupt or jump to answer questions you know are coming—the other party could think you're belittling them.

If you're concerned you'll be perceived as too young, you need to convey predictability and a respect for traditions. Arrive early and enter a room with a bit of solemnity. There's no need to be sullen, just serious. Don't sit until invited to do so by the other party—that shows old world manners. Smiling is fine at first, but settle into a sober professional demeanor as soon as possible. Make and maintain eye contact as often as possible, and you'll send a message of earnestness. Try not to shift your position very often. Sit with your body back in your seat, and when asked a question slightly tilt your head to a side while maintaining eye contact—that's read as being duly but not overly attentive. Don't touch your face or look down at any time; both convey a lack of confidence. Answer all questions without very much hesitation to show you're on top of your material. Never act surprised, even if you are. Try to be as matter-of-fact as you can. You want the other party to feel that, despite your age, this isn't the first time you've been in this kind of situation.

Finally, choose language that reinforces the rest of your age camouflage. If you're worried about being too old, you don't need to talk like a hip hopper or rap artist, just avoid backward looking words or phrases. Never say things like, "in my experience," "in the past," or "at Acme we used to. . . ." In fact, try to banish the past tense from your language altogether. Instead use phrases such as "one solution might be," or "have you considered. . . ." Don't ask about specifics that assume a positive outcome to the meeting. For example, in an initial job interview don't ask questions about salary, benefits, and certainly not about retirement plans. Instead, ask questions that presuppose this won't be your last job, such as "what is the future career path you envision for the person who fills this position;" or "what do you see as the evolving challenges that will be facing the person you hire?"

If you're worried about seeming too young, make sure your language indicates prudence and thoughtfulness. You can do that by speaking in complete, complex sentences rather than fragments. One good tip is to begin by rephrasing or rewording the other party's question. For example, "In response to your question about how I would manage a technological transition. . . ." If you're lacking relevant experience of your own to answer a question, feel free to draw on others' experiences or case studies you've read. That will turn a perceived weakness (lack of experience) into a perceived strength (industry knowledge). For instance, you could say something like, "one possible solution to that could be to try the same type of shift in marketing as Apple Computer successfully executed in 1998." Ask specific questions that show pragmatism. Feel free to ask about salary, benefits, and other forms of compensation. In order to keep from seeming presumptuous, you can use phrases such as, "what is the range of compensation you'd be offering the person who fills this position?"

I hope you don't come away from this chapter feeling you need to somehow be dishonest to break down age barriers. I certainly don't advocate lying, either about your age or your abilities. But I do think it's important to package yourself well. Age bias has nothing to do with reality and everything to do with perceptions. I believe the most successful way to battle misperceptions, bias, and stereotypes is to turn the kind of intellectual laziness such attitudes represent to your advantage. If someone tends to make snap judgments, simply make sure you provide him or her with the signals that will lead to snap judgments in your favor. Send the right signals, and age will no longer be a closed door blocking you from living the life of your dreams.

CHAPTER 6

Money:
A Question of Choice

"Wealth is not without its advantages and the case to the contrary,
although it has often been made, has never proved widely persuasive."

—JOHN KENNETH GALBRAITH

Money can transform a strenuous uphill climb of a Second Act into a leisurely stroll. But you probably suspected that already. After all, you're reading this chapter because you feel money is an obstacle to your Second Act. Well, I have good news and bad news.

First the bad news: Money really does matter. A lot. No amount of spiritual enlightenment or psychological counseling is going to change that. Money may not buy you happiness... but it sure helps. A lack of money can bring you *unhappiness*, both through physical deprivations—not having sufficient food, clothing, or shelter—and psychological pain—not measuring up to standards of success. Let's be honest: Money *can* buy you things, which in turn provide temporal joy if not spiritual bliss. It may not be able to buy you health, but it can get you the best medical care. It may not be able to buy you love, but it certainly makes it easier to get dates. And, although money may not automatically give you the life of your dreams, it does make the journey there a lot more manageable. For instance, it's a lot easier starting over in an entry-level job if you don't need to worry about paying for your kid's braces. Having sufficient money will let you launch your Second Act sooner and with less strain.

Now the good news: Of the twelve general barriers to Second Acts, money is actually the easiest to overcome. Sound's crazy, I know. Most people think the opposite is the case: That money is the toughest barrier to a Second Act. But it's not. Let me explain.

IT'S ENTIRELY UP TO YOU

Overcoming money obstacles is a matter of choice. After meeting our most rudimentary requirements for food, clothing, and shelter, everything else we spend is by choice.

You (and your family if you have one) choose the kind of home in which you live. You, your spouse, and your child can decide to rent a two-bedroom moderately priced apartment in an average part of town. Entertaining at home might be difficult. Storage could be at a minimum. And, the aesthetics might not enthrall. However, it could only cost you 20 percent of your income. Alternatively, the three of you could choose to own a four-bedroom home on a 1/2 acre lot in an affluent part of town. Your guests could have their own bedroom and bathroom. The kitchen might be fit for a gourmet chef. And it could look like it came straight out of *Architectural Digest*. But, it could cost you as much as 60 percent of your income.

You make the same choices about other parts of your life as well. Do you go out to dinner five times a week or once a month? Maybe you're wearing the latest fashions, or you might have on clothes from when Reagan was president. There could be a state-of-the-art audio-video system in your den, that fully integrates with the satellite on your roof and the latest generation computer

---

Famous Second Act

MICHAEL MILKEN

Michael Milken's first act didn't just end, it crashed. When he admitted to fraud and racketeering charges in April 1989, it represented a dramatic reversal in fortune. But that wasn't the first turnaround in his life. Previously, he had gone from being a young boy helping his accountant father prepare tax returns in their suburban Los Angeles home, to being the billionaire poster boy for the use of high-risk, high-yield bonds in financing corporate takeovers. He and the firm for which he worked, Drexel, Burnham, Lambert, became synonymous with "junk

and digital imaging products in your office. Or, you could still be using an old television with a set of rabbit ears and a boom box you bought when you were in college. Are you planning for your daughter to go to Harvard, or are you counting on her attending community college and then State U? The list of choices is huge, going down as far as whether you opt to have filet mignon or pasta when you go out for dinner.

And, your money choices aren't just about spending either. You've a great deal of control over your revenue stream as well. Granted, your control over your income isn't total, as it is with your expenses, but it's greater than most initially believe. What do you do with your old dining room set when you buy a replacement? You could leave it by the side of the road for the trash man, give it to one of your adult children, donate it to the Salvation Army and get a tax deduction (thus cutting your expenses), or you could sell it at a yard sale or on eBay (increasing your revenue).

bonds." Soon after being freed from prison in 1993, Milken learned he had prostate cancer and was given 18 months to live. He fought his illness, and in the process, launched a Second Act. The man who hosted the infamous "Predator's Ball" junk bond conference went on a strict low-fat near vegetarian diet and started meditating. He became a spokesman and fund raiser for prostate cancer charities, raising more than $63 million for prostate cancer research, and publishing a cookbook (*The Taste for Living Cookbook: Mike Milken's Favorite Recipes for Fighting Cancer*). He also started a "cradle-to-grave learning company" called Knowledge Universe with the help of his younger brother and Oracle's Larry Ellison. ■

Maybe you've turned down freelance work because you didn't want to work on the weekend. Perhaps you didn't go after a promotion because it would entail longer hours. Could you work a part-time job at night? Savings in a money market fund or certificate of deposit aren't earning as much for you as, say, a bond fund or an annuity. Fully own your own home? A reverse mortgage could turn your equity into a tax-free income.

This isn't going to be a chapter all about making sacrifices because, as you'll see, I don't think you need to experience pain to overcome your money obstacles. But you will need to make choices. That's why the important thing to focus on now is that you really do have control over money. Turn your money decisions into conscious choices, not reflexive acts, and you'll be in the right frame of mind to overcome your money obstacles. Let's take on the simplest of those obstacles first: money as an internal obstacle.

TURNING YOUR INTERNAL BARRIER INTO AN EXTERNAL BARRIER

If you characterized money as an internal barrier on your CLOSED DOORS list, it's because you assumed, for instance, your family couldn't cope with the 40 percent cut in your income that would result from your becoming a school teacher. You didn't actually run the numbers to see what would be the impact of leaving your job with the bank. You have a feeling, a hunch, a strong sense, or a suspicion. But you don't have the facts. The way to overcome this internal obstacle is simply to turn it into an external obstacle. You do that by actually running the numbers. That begins with the first exercise in this chapter.

Even if you already know money will be a problem, and originally characterized it as an external barrier, I'd like you to start with the first exercise anyway. That's because I'll be helping you generate a very detailed analysis of your income and expenses. A comprehensive breakdown will be vital in subsequent exercises in which you'll be addressing your deficits. However, if you're truly obsessive about your finances, I'll let you jump forward to the subhead "Overcoming External Money Barriers" later in this chapter. Here's the test: without peeking, tell me how much money is in your wallet. Then, tell me how much cash you spent this week, and what you spent it on. If you can't come up with those answers in less than five minutes, you're not obsessive enough to skip the next two exercises.

"WHAT AM I SPENDING?"

There was a reason I asked about cash. I've found most people can't account for almost 60 percent of the cash they spend. The ubiquitous Automated Teller Machines have made it so easy to get cash any time you need it, most people don't think twice

Famous Second Act

SONNY BONO

Salvatore Bono had more than his share of Second Acts. Born in Detroit, Michigan, his Sicilian immigrant parents moved the family to Los Angeles when he was seven. He dropped out of high school and began writing songs while working as a waiter, construction worker, and butcher's assistant. Bono was eventually able to land work as a producer and songwriter. At the age of twenty-eight, he met and married Cherilyn La Pierre and began managing her career. His initial Second Act came when he and his wife, performing as a duo known firstly as Caeser and Cleo and then as Sonny and Cher, had an international hit with "I Got You Babe," a song Bono wrote, arranged, and produced. After a period on top of the charts, their careers waned until 1971 when they had another Second Act, turning themselves into a television comedy team as well as a performing duo. Their show ran for four years. After divorcing from Cher, Bono tried others Second Acts: acting on television and running restaurants. But a more successful Second Act was to follow when he successfully ran for mayor of Palm Springs, California, and then, in 1994, won a seat in Congress. He was re-elected in 1996 but died in a skiing accident before his second term was completed. ■

about reaching into their pocket for greenbacks. When the wad starts getting small, we just head over to the nearest bank, or mall, or even gas station, insert a bank card in the machine, and more money comes out. Perhaps there are still some folks out there besides me who remember we used to need to cash a check to get cash. Sure, it wasn't convenient to have to wait on line to get money. It meant altering your schedule to fit the bank's hours. And most of all, it required thought and planning. On pay day, you had to figure out how much cash you'd need until your next paycheck. The perception was you had a finite amount of cash. Today, with ATMs being so convenient, the perception is you have an infinite amount of cash. In order to figure out whether or not money really is an obstacle to your Second Act, you first need to determine *exactly* what you're spending each month. That's going to require tracking your cash much more closely.

Exercise 1

Buy yourself a small note pad; one that fits in your pocket, purse, or briefcase. It should be light enough that you can carry it with you everywhere. If it has a loop for a pen or pencil, all the better. Starting the first day of the month after you purchase it, start recording everything you spend in cash. You don't need to keep track of pennies; just round everything to the nearest dollar. (Round $.50 up to $1.) And, don't worry about categorizing the expenses just yet. You're going to track all your cash expenditures for ninety days. Only then will you categorize them. Now, simply make a note of the date, the amount, and what it was for. For instance, a day's worth of entries might look like this:

8/1	coffee @ Starbucks	$ 4
8/1	newspaper @ stand	$ 1
8/1	lunch @ deli	$12
8/1	gas for car	$18
8/1	bridge toll	$ 2
8/1	video rental	$ 4

Next, I want you to go to an office supply store and purchase an accounting pad that provides space for at least three columns of figures. Don't forget to make a note of what you spent. When you get home, turn to a blank page on the accounting pad. Title the page REGULAR EXPENSES. In the memo column, you're going to start listing categories for things on which you regularly spend money. By regularly, I mean at least four times a year. Obviously, everyone spends money differently, but here's a sample list you can draw from that I think is quite comprehensive:

primary rent/mortgage	gifts
secondary rent/mortgage	day care/baby sitting
equity loan payments	toys/activity fees
student loan payments	school supplies
personal loan payments	movies/videos/plays/etc.
parent/child rent subsidies	personal dining out
child's college tuition	work lunches out
child's private school tuition	greens fees/court rentals
continuing education	hobbies/craft
utilities (gas, oil, electric)	newspapers/magazines
trash disposal	books/videos/DVDs/CDs
telephone	photo film and processing
cellular telephone	blank videos/floppies/CDs
internet connection	prescriptions
cable television	medical fees
satellite television	nonprescription drugs
water	groceries
state estimated taxes	wine and spirits
federal estimated taxes	household supplies
gardening/plowing service	personal care products
house cleaning service	personal care services

counseling fees	tolls
dry cleaning/laundry	transportation fares
clothing for work/school	computer software
clothing for home/play	web site subscriptions
pet food	retirement savings
pet medications	college savings
pet grooming	other savings
auto payments	health insurance
auto fuel	home insurance
auto maintenance	credit card debt service
parking	installment debt payments

Now, turn to a blank page on the accounting pad and title it IRREGULAR EXPENSES. These are things you spend money on once, twice, or three times a year; or expenses which are unpredictable. Once again, start writing relevant categories in the memo section of the page. Here's another list to get you started:

unreimbursable medical bills	computer equipment
auto repairs	exercise/sports equipment
house repairs	health club memberships
major house maintenance	social club memberships
appliance repairs	professional dues
charitable contributions	home office supplies
home furnishings	tools
housewares	jewelry
landscaping/plantings	art work
audio equipment	collectibles
photo equipment	local taxes
video equipment	state taxes

federal taxes	pet boarding
professional fees	veterinary bills
vacation travel	life insurance
vacation meals	auto insurance
vacation lodging	disability insurance
vacation souvenirs	long-term care insurance
summer camp fees	personal loans

Now comes the hard part: You're going to fill in all those blank columns.

Turn back to the pages titled REGULAR EXPENSES. Head the first of the numeric columns Month 1, the second Month 2, and the third Month 3.

Let's tackle your noncash spending.

If you always hated clutter and haven't kept any records of your past expenses now you're going to need to start. Buy yourself three file folders and preserve all your check stubs, credit card receipts, and bank statements for the next three months. At that point, you'll have enough records to at least get started.

If you're a pack rat type, and keep all your receipts, check stubs, and credit card statements organized, congratulations. You'll be able to immediately reconstruct your noncash spending patterns based on your past. It will probably take you at least two full days, so set aside either one or two weekends.

Clear off the kitchen or dining room table. Get out a calculator, your accounting pad, and a pencil with an eraser. Make yourself a pot of coffee. Bring your files of receipts, statements, and checks up from the basement or out of the file cabinet. Label one blank page on your accounting pad for each of the categories listed on your REGULAR EXPENSES pages. Once again, label the three numeric columns Month 1, Month 2, and Month 3.

Pull out the receipts, statements, and check stubs from the previous month.[19] Go through the records, one by one, noting the amount spent on in the first monthly column of the page you've dedicated to that category of expense. Don't worry about the pennies. Just round to the nearest dollar. Go through all the monthly receipts, statements, and stubs.

Repeat the process with the receipts for the two previous months, putting the numbers in the proper monthly column on each category page.

(One quick tip about how to treat credit card bills. If you are in the habit of fully paying off your card balance every month, simply assign the individual charges on the bills to the proper categories. However, if you've kept a balance and typically pay either a set amount or the minimum due, list that number under credit card debt service, rather than trying to categorize the individual charges from prior months. However, add all the current charges to the individual categories.)

With the individual category pages filled in, total up each column. Then, transfer those totals to the corresponding lines and columns on your REGULAR EXPENSES pages. Use a pencil, because you're going to need to change some of them soon.

While you're probably sick of the process by now, please take a minute to check the numbers over. You're going to be basing some important decisions on the results of this and subsequent exercises so being as accurate as possible is in your own best inter-

---

[19] I hate to tell you, but if you haven't organized your receipts and check stubs by month you're going to need to do it now. Sure it's a pain, but you've got to start some time, and there's no time better than now, when you have a terrific reason for doing it: You're going after the life of your dreams. Besides, you're still better off than someone who hasn't kept any receipts or stubs. They'll be doing this for another three months.

ests. Do any of the numbers seem strange or just not feel right? Maybe the gift total seems particularly low. That could be because there were no birthdays, anniversaries, or major holidays in the past three months. Perhaps the numbers for your child's activity fees are unusually high. Is it because you chose three summer months, or a season when your child is very active in an expensive sport? If you notice any glaring discrepancies like these, try to compensate for them. For instance, total up your gift spending for December and use that as one of the three monthly figures.[20] Or, you could use just one of the months when your child's activity fees are high, and use two other more typical monthly subtotals for the other columns.

In addition, go over the list of expenses with an eye toward any which you feel may increase due to your launching a Second Act. For instance, if you currently don't travel for work but your dream involves shifting to a career that will require commuting, estimate what your added transportation, auto, parking, and toll expenses will be by checking out the costs. If you'll need to go back to school, you may incur student loans. Call the educational institution to get an idea of the tuition costs, and then telephone someone at your bank to get a rough estimate of what monthly loan payments for that amount might be. Increase your current monthly expenditures to match your projected future expenses.

If you were able to come up with your noncash totals by reconstructing your records, you can now set the accounting pad aside for three months. During that time, concentrate on keeping track of your cash spending in your little notepad, and work on overcoming some of the other barriers to your Second Act.

---

[20] For those with large families or who are swept up by the Christmas spirit, this is probably a good thing to do whether or not the initial numbers seem wrong.

Once you have a record of three months of your cash spending, it's time to rerun the numbers. Clear off the table again. Make sure you've fresh batteries in your calculator and your pencils are sharpened. Instead of a pot of coffee you can just make a cup. This won't take as long as your previous session—probably just an afternoon or morning. And take out your Second Act notebook as well.

In your little notepad, total up the cash you spent on each category in the first month you tracked. Turn back to the pages in your accounting pad titled REGULAR EXPENSES. Find the line where you've recorded three monthly subtotals of noncash spending on that category. Using your calculator, add the number from your little notepad to the subtotal you earlier recorded in the accounting pad for the first month. Erase the old number and write in your new total. This is an estimate of your combined cash and noncash spending. Repeat the process for all three months and every category.

Now it's time to come up with some averages. Open up your trusty Second Act notebook and turn to a fresh page. Title it REGULAR MONTHLY EXPENSES. Add up the monthly totals for each category and divide by three to come up with an average. Write the name of the category along with that average in your notebook. Finish up your coffee, put your materials away, and take a week off.[21] Go out and spend some cash without keeping track of it—just not too much because you've still got work to do. You need to come up with a similar list of your irregular expenses.

---

[21] Make sure you save all your worksheets, including the pages from your accounting pad and your little cash notepad. They might come in handy if you need to recalculate your numbers based on changes resulting from your working to open other closed doors.

If you're a good record keeper you can figure out your irregular expenses in a weekend afternoon. Bring your now familiar set of supplies to the kitchen table. Turn to the pages in the accounting pad you previously labeled IRREGULAR EXPENSES and filled with the appropriate categories. Label the first numeric column ANNUAL, the second QUARTERLY, and the third MONTHLY.

Search through your check stubs and credit card statements, starting in January, for records of these expenditures. Go through the folders, month by month, pulling out all the records that apply to your search. Organize them by category. When you've gone through the whole year, come up with some annual totals. Write those numbers in the appropriate places on your IRREGU-LAR EXPENSES pages. Work your way through each category until you've filled in the entire first column.

(One important aside: If you're someone that, for whatever reason, pays cash for major expenses, it's essential you try to reconstruct those expenditures, even if it's just from memory. Whether you wanted a record of them or not, it's important to account for them in this exercise. Remember you're doing this for yourself and your family, not the IRS.)

When you've completed the first column, take out your calcu-lator. Divide the annual total for each category by four and write the result in the second column. labeled QUARTERLY. Divide the annual total for each category by 12 and write that result in the third column, labeled MONTHLY.

If you haven't kept good records, coming up with your num-bers will be a bit more time consuming. Think of it as a week long project that you'll do on your lunch hour, in the evening, and on the weekend. Pull out your IRREGULAR EXPENSES pages. Go down the list of items, and on a separate piece of scrap paper, note where you can find out how much each costs. For example, you could contact your insurance agents for information on the premiums for your life, auto, and other policies. A telephone call to your accountant can yield how much you've paid in taxes the previous three years. For those categories, such as home repairs or vacation expenses, where there isn't a single source you'll need to try to reconstruct what you've spent the past year. Speak with your family and friends so you're drawing on more than just your memory. Obviously, in the end, you'll be making general estimates. But if you lack any documentation or a good source for the information that's all you can do. While you're getting annoyed at having to wait for return telephone calls, or at having to try to remember how much it cost you to fix the washing machine, resolve to keep better records in the future.

With the IRREGULAR EXPENSES pages in your accounting pad complete, you can turn back to your Second Act notebook. Label a fresh page IRREGULAR MONTHLY EXPENSES and write down each category and the corresponding figure in the monthly column. Next, turn to another fresh page and, on three separate lines, write total regular monthly expenses, total irregular monthly expenses, and total monthly expenses. Take out your calculator and add up all the numbers on your regular and irregular expense lists. Transfer the numbers to your notebook. Add them together and write down the result.

Give yourself a pat on the back. Pour yourself a nice glass of wine, or have a Krispy Kreme as a reward. You've now accomplished something very few ever do: You've determined both how much you spend and where your money goes. This information may have been a pain to acquire, but it provides you with incredible power. First, it lets you know exactly how much money you need to continue to earn in order to maintain your current standard of living. Second, and perhaps most importantly, it provides you with details you need to make informed decisions. Remember, almost all spending is a choice. You now have, in black and white, the grounds for making future choices. If you find your Second Act won't provide you with the funds you need to maintain your current lifestyle, you can now go through your expenditures, category by category, and look for places where you're willing to make sacrifices in order to lead the life of your dreams. (That's what Exercise 4 is all about.)

But before you get worried about what those sacrifices may entail, let's make sure they're really necessary.

WHAT WILL MY INCOME BE?

You're now halfway toward knowing, rather than just assuming, whether or not money will be an obstacle to your Second Act. The next step is to determine whether your income will be sufficient to cover your now fully analyzed expenses.

Exercise 2

Take out your Second Act notebook and turn to your MISSION STATEMENT. Ask yourself, "Where will my income be coming from if my dream becomes real?"

Let's say you're married, you and your spouse both work, and your dream is to have a child and stay home full time to raise it for at least five years. In that scenario your earned income would come from your spouse's job.[22] Perhaps you're single and your dream is to give up your job as a staff reporter at a daily newspaper and become a freelance writer. That means your earned income would be from the fees you earned. It could be your

---

[22] Earned income is just that: money you earn from your labors, usually in the form of fees, salary, or wages. Unearned income is money from passive actives, such as investing or saving.

J. K. ROWLING

Joanne Kathleen Rowling was in desperate need of a Second Act. At age 25 she had moved to Portugal to teach English. While there, Rowling married and had a child. But when her marriage ended in divorce she picked up her daughter and moved to Edinburgh, Scotland, to be near her younger sister. Living on public assistance and struggling to support herself and her daughter, she was overjoyed when she finally sold her first book for approximately $4,000. Her Second Act was launched. By 1999 the first three installments in her Harry Potter series of children's books had claimed the top three slots

dream is to change careers from being an art teacher to a web page designer. Obviously your earned income would then come from your new job. Turn to a fresh page in your notebook, title it INCOME SOURCES, and write up a brief description of from where your money will be coming.

If you'll be relying on an already existing stream of income, such as your current salary or a spouse's present earnings, you can simply write that number down after the description. Did you include deductions from this income stream in your list of expenses—say the monthly contributions you make to a 401(k) or for health insurance? In that case, record the gross amount. Otherwise, write down the net income.

If you'll be living on a new stream of income, you'll need to do some research to estimate what it will be. Up until recently this was a difficult task, one requiring a great many telephone calls to

on *The New York Times* bestseller list. In July 2000, the fourth volume in the series, *Harry Potter and the Goblet of Fire*, became the fastest selling book in history. By that time, the first three books in the series had earned around $480 million in just three years. There are thirty-five million copies in print in thirty-five languages. In November 2001, the screen adaptation of the first book, *Harry Potter and the Sorcerer's Stone*, opened on a record number of screens—8,200—and had the largest opening weekend sales in history, about $93.5 million. One month later, Rowling, now one of the wealthiest women in the United Kingdom, married Dr. Neil Murray. She plans to write a total of seven Harry Potter books. ■

headhunters, employment agencies, and professional associations and trips to the library to dig up stories in obscure trade publications. Today all you need is to go online.

Start your search at the Bureau of Labor Statistics Occupational Outlook Handbook (http://stats.bls.gov/oco/home.htm). There, you'll find an alphabetical listing of occupations to search through. Click on the listing that best matches your planned new career and you'll find a web page containing

- Significant points about the job
- A discussion of the nature of the work
- A description of the typical working conditions
- The job's traditional employment conditions
- The preferred or usual training and education
- Other qualifications and advancement potential

- The current job outlook
- Average earnings
- Related occupations
- Sources of additional information

It's a terrific site with a wealth of useful information for those planning a Second Act. In fact, I'd suggest you bookmark the site. Print out the pages describing your proposed new job, and transfer the earnings information, which is probably expressed in a range, to the INCOME SOURCES page in your Second Act notebook.

Next, click over to JobStar Central (http://jobstar.org/tools/salary/sal-prof.cfm), an online job search guide that offers links to more than 300 online profession-specific salary surveys. This one site provides the kind of information it used to take weeks to collect. In addition to its own linked surveys JobStar provides connections to additional sites for other profession-specific salary information. Print out these results as well and add the salary range information you've learned to your Second Act notebook.

A third site that's helpful is Salary.com (http://www.salary.com), which has a very useful calculator it calls "The Salary Wizard." By selecting a job category and then inputting your ZIP code or your metropolitan area, it will provide you with a more regional specific salary range. You can enter even more data to refine the results further and get a more personalized result. While, of necessity, it draws its results from a smaller sample than the other two sites, I think that's balanced by its sharper geographic focus. Once again, print out your findings and add the range to your notebook.

At this point you'll need to reconcile and combine the three different ranges you've discovered. My suggestion is to rewrite the results as the largest possible range, by picking the highest figure cited as your new top and the lowest figure cited as your new bottom. Divide these numbers by 12 to come up with a monthly income range, and write that down in your Second Act notebook as well.

Don't jump to any conclusions and immediately compare this range to the expense estimates you came up with in Exercise 1. You need to factor in two more elements before you can make an accurate judgment: transition time and unearned income.

Give some thought to whether or not you can assume a seamless transition to this new income stream. Obviously, if your Second Act involves shifting from two incomes to one, or from one job to another, there needn't be any transitionary period. (I'm hoping you've taken to heart Building Block 6 and are going to practice bifocal vision. That means not quitting your current job until you've one in your new career already lined up.) But if your Second Act requires some type of training or education, you may need to factor study time into your financial decisions. There are all sorts of ways to shorten or even eliminate this transition period, and I'll discuss them in Chapters 7 and 10. But for now, let's say you want to shift from being an insurance adjuster to a public school teacher, and you believe it will require you to go back to college full time for six months. That means you'll need to set aside sufficient funds to cover your monthly expenses for six months, after which you'd be bringing in your new income. Multiply your estimate of monthly expenses by the number of months you think you'll need to do without an income. Make a note of this number on your INCOME SOURCES page, labeling it TRANSITION RESERVE. This may never actually be an issue, depending on the results of the exercises in Chapters 7 and 10, but it's prudent to at least account for the possibility at this stage.

Finally, you need to factor in your unearned income. Do you have savings or nonqualified investments that generate interest income?[23] Maybe you receive a regular annual $5,000 gift from your grandmother. Perhaps your parents left you a rental property that provides you with a tidy $10,000 a year profit. Make

note of any such unearned income and write them down on your
INCOME SOURCES page. Total up the numbers, and divide the
result by 12 to come up with a monthly estimate of unearned
income. Write this down in your notebook as well, calling the figure monthly unearned income.

Now, add your unearned income estimates to both the top and
bottom of the projected salary range you developed earlier. Label
the number monthly income range. How does it compare to the
total monthly expense figure you came up with in Exercise 17? In
order to be conservative and give yourself the greatest margin for
error, I think you should focus on the lowest figure in the range.

If the lowest figure in your monthly income range is above
your expense estimate, money will definitely *not* be a long-term
obstacle to your Second Act.

If the lowest figure in your monthly income range is above
your monthly expense estimate, but you potentially need to come
up with a transition reserve, money *may* be a short-term obstacle.
That will depend on whether you can cut or eliminate that training time, or if you currently have sufficient savings to carry you
through the transition period. If you have enough in the bank to
pay your expenses while you, say, go back to school, money isn't
an obstacle for you. If you don't have enough savings to tide you
over, money is a short-term obstacle. You'll need to work on cutting the time required in Chapters 7 and 10. But you'll also need
to work on raising the savings by increasing your income and/or
cutting your expenses. Estimate how much money you will need

---

[23] By nonqualified investments I mean investments that are taxable as opposed to
those in IRAs, 401(k)s, Keoghs, or SEPs, which are tax deferred. The income
from tax-deferred investments won't be of help to you now unless you're
already old enough to draw from such retirement plans. If you are, consider the
income as coming from nonqualified sources.

as a transition reserve and write that number down in your Second Act notebook. Reaching it will be your goal in the remaining two exercises of the chapter.

If the lowest figure in your monthly income range is below your monthly expense estimate, money is definitely a barrier to living the life of your dreams. But, like all barriers to Second Acts, it can be overcome. Subtract your projected monthly income from your estimated monthly expenses. The result is your monthly deficit. Write it down in your Second Act notebook. Multiply it by 12 and write that number down as well, labeling it "annual deficit." Your goal for the rest of this chapter is to eliminate this shortfall.

OVERCOMING EXTERNAL
MONEY BARRIERS

Maybe you're lucky, and actually running the numbers has allayed your fears about money being an obstacle. Perhaps you're not spending as much as you thought. Maybe the income you're likely to earn from your Second Act is higher than you anticipated. In either case, give a sigh of relief. But before you go on to the chapter dealing with the next obstacle on your CLOSED DOORS page, I'd like to make a suggestion: Why not go through the rest of the exercises in this chapter anyway?

By figuring out ways to cut your expenses and increase your income you'll expand the financial cushion you've just discovered. A larger surplus will give you the freedom to be more selective in your choices of revenue streams and more liberal in your spending decisions. Extra money will also provide you with more time to bring your Second Act to fruition. I strongly encourage you to at least read the rest of this chapter. You've already done the two hardest exercises. If you don't think the cost cutting and money making ideas I offer are worth the efforts required, I won't argue with you.

If you ran all the numbers and have discovered money will indeed be an obstacle, congratulations: You've succeeded in turning an internal problem into an external one. That's good because external barriers are easier to overcome. You've now got a twofold mission. First, you need to find ways to increase your revenue stream. And second, you must look for places where you can cut your expenses. I know both prospects sound as appealing as having root canal work done on your teeth. I'll be honest with you: neither of these two tasks is a piece of cake. But at the same time, they're not the ordeals you may imagine. You've probably read piles of books and countless articles about saving money by bringing your lunch to work or turning down your thermostat. The advice I'll be offering is a bit different, however. I think you'll find I've got some relatively painless ideas that can both produce and save surprising sums.[24]

HOW CAN I INCREASE REVENUES?

When faced with a deficit, the instinctive reaction is to look to cut expenses. That's true of individuals, businesses, and Republican administrations. I'm not sure why this is the reflex, though I suspect it has to do with feelings of guilt. On some level it's felt that deficits could only have come through profligacy, so the only proper response is self punishment. Setting aside both psychology and politics, I think the smartest—and certainly the least painful—first response to a deficit is to look to increase revenues

---

[24] Out of necessity, the information I'm providing in this chapter is concise. For a fuller explanation of all these concepts I'd suggest you take a look at my own *Die Broke Complete Guide to Money* (HarperCollins, 2000).

rather than cut expenses. There are a number of ways you can do that.

(Throughout this process keep your deficit number in mind. Follow as many income increasing options as you need to close your deficit. Once you've closed the gap and/or have acquired enough for your reserve you can be a bit more relaxed about enacting the rest of the ideas. Still, the more money in your pocket the better, especially because many of the techniques are painless. I'd urge you to at least read all the options.)

1. *Ask for a raise.* The most time consuming, but least painful and most effective way to increase your income is, not surprisingly, to ask your employer for an increase. That's true even if your Second Act involves an eventual change in career or job. The more money you get in your pocket before you leave the better. Besides, a higher exiting salary at your old job could lead to a higher starting salary at your new job.

   To maximize both the odds of your getting a raise and the size of the pay hike, you'll need to start working on it three months in advance. Ignore the normal date of your annual salary review. That way you'll bypass the practiced stinginess of human resources departments and will catch your superior without a prepared rejection. Instead, circle a date just after what you expect to be a major accomplishment, such as the completion of a big project. That's the moment when your value will be highest and most obvious.

   Start sprucing up your image. If you haven't already, start imitating the level (but not style) of dress of the individual you'll be approaching for a raise. Mimic his or her hours as well, except get in a couple of minutes earlier and leave a couple of minutes later. The idea is to make yourself appear omnipresent. Make sure your expressions and mannerisms convey someone who is optimistic, eager, and determined. Avoid the water cooler, coffee machine, lunch room, and any other place where people gather to gossip and bitch. You don't want to be seen doing anything other than working.

Put together an achievement memo. List all the ways you've boosted the bottom line by cutting costs, increasing revenue, or saving time. Note all the new accounts you've lined up, assigning each a specific dollar amount. ("Closed Widget Inc. account, bringing in $23,500 annually.") Similarly, record any improvements you've made to existing accounts, specifically noting the percentage improvement. ("Boosted return on Acme portfolio, resulting in fee increase of 12 percent.") Include any ways you've grown the business, including new products, strategies, affiliations, and services.

Conduct a salary survey of your own position, using the same techniques outlined in Exercise 2. Put the results in a memo separate from your achievement memo. This salary survey memo should document your conclusion that, based on your survey, you're underpaid. Explain the sources of your numbers; that will give them more credence.

Two weeks before your chosen date, make an appointment for your meeting. Avoid Mondays, which are too busy, and Fridays, when minds quickly turn to thoughts of the weekend. The best time is early, before normal working hours, making it clear this is an important meeting outside the ordinary routine.

On the night before your meeting prepare a script, including dialog and stage directions. Walk in briskly, make direct eye contact, shake hands firmly, and before even sitting down, thank your boss for the role he or she has played in your career up until now. Then immediately say, "but I have a problem I need your help with." Sit down, make direct eye contact again, and say something like, "I've found my salary no longer reflects my contribution to the company." Hand over your achievement memo, saying, "Here's a brief memo outlining my contributions." Then add that you've "been so busy concentrating on your work that you haven't given enough attention to your salary." Follow this comment by handing over your salary survey memo, saying that according to the research you've done, you'll "need an increase in order to keep pace."

If your boss disputes your numbers, ask for suggestions for further research and another appointment in two weeks to review your new findings. If he or she asks whether you're looking for another job say you "haven't initiated contact" but that you're often approached. . . as you're sure he or she is as well. Stress you're committed to the company. . . as well as to keeping pace with your peers. If you're met with pleas of poverty, agree to a deferred increase with retroactive payments. If your boss wants to start negotiating specific numbers try to avoid being the first to offer a number. If you throw out a figure it can only be negotiated down. If he or she breaks the ice it can only go up.

If all your efforts fail, it's a sign it's time to find a new job, whether or not it was originally part of your Second Act.

2. *Take a part-time job.* If your raise doesn't yield enough to eliminate your deficit or generate a sufficient transition reserve, consider taking a second, part-time job to bring in more income.

This second job shouldn't be related to either your full-time job or your Second Act. You don't want any conflicts of interest, with your employer or yourself. If in an effort to overcome another obstacle, such as a lack of training or experience, you choose to ease into your Second Act by taking a part-time job, that's different. But your goal right now is strictly financial. Steer clear of positions that compensate through commission. They'll force you to work longer hours and dedicate more of your energies to the job then you should. Other than that caveat, don't let your ego get in the way of doing honest labor of any kind. Show up on time, work hard, collect your paycheck, and don't bring work home with you. Your moonlighting is a way to bring in extra money, nothing more.

3. *Increase your rates*. Employees know they must ask for a raise to get more money. But sometimes the self employed forget that option. Instead of increasing their rates, they focus on landing additional clients or customers.

   If you are self employed and you haven't raised your fees in the past year, you're losing ground to inflation. Send out a letter announcing a fee increase now. Blame it on the increased cost of doing business. That's something every client will be able to understand.

   Assume 50 percent of your clients will accept the increase without batting an eye. Twenty five percent will call to negotiate. Try to work out a compromise with these hagglers, but don't fall all the way back to your original fee. That will set the precedent that all future efforts at rate increases can be negotiated away. The remaining 25 percent will threaten to bolt. Express your desire to keep them. Indicate your willingness to compromise, but stress circumstances are beyond your control. Don't back down.

If you're good at what you do, most of these rebelling clients will find a way to stay on board.

4. *Collect your inheritance early.* Do you know of an inheritance coming your way in the next decade or so? You can approach your benefactor and ask for the gift now, when you could really use it. If they speed up the gift you can thank them in person and they can get the added pleasure of seeing how their largesse enabled your lifelong happiness.

It's vital you have a specific number in mind—enough, say, to cover your monthly deficit for two years—and that you know at least that much money has already been set aside for you. Be contrite, humble, and grateful for the existence of the gift, without assuming it will be delivered ahead of schedule. Have a description prepared about how this early inheritance will improve the quality of your life. Explain all the efforts you've made to boost your income and cut costs.

Don't have this conversation within six months of having bought yourself any luxury item or of having gone on an expensive vacation. Try to have the talk on the weekend at your benefactor's home, reinforcing the closeness of your relationship. If the benefactors are a couple—your grandparents, for instance—speak first with the one you think will be more reluctant. That way you know you'll only need to go through the process once, and you'll avoid creating a conflict between them. The tougher one will make an overpowering ally if you get him or her to come around.

Never get angry or project a sense of entitlement. Your goal is to get the money to launch your Second Act, so it's better to grovel a bit and be ashamed than it is to maintain your pride and remain stuck in an unhappy life. If your request is granted, thank them profusely and promise to keep them abreast of the progress of your Second Act. If your request is turned down, thank them profusely for hearing you out. Reiterate your unconditional love for them. Make sure to call again within the month and ask after them, without mentioning the request. Stay in regular contact, but never raise the issue. Over time your silence will speak louder than any words could. If nothing else, it will guarantee you still eventually get the inheritance.

5. *Convert assets to cash.* If you have some valuable unused or underused assets it's relatively painless these days to convert them into cash. Such a one shot influx of funds might not have much of an impact on your monthly deficit. But it could provide a nice chunk of cash for your transition reserve.

Do you have an expensive camera outfit you haven't used since the kids got out of diapers? You'd be surprised what classic photo equipment—particularly medium format, Nikon, and Leica cameras—can fetch on eBay. Go through your basement, garage and attic. Old books, hand tools, weapons, toys, records, and magazines all seem to attract obsessive collectors willing to overspend online.

Go through your family heirlooms as well. Are your mother's diamonds sitting unused on top of your dresser or in your safe deposit box? Perhaps there's an antique sideboard gathering dust in your guest room. While it's tough to place a price on sentimental value you need to try. Is having the heirloom worth more than living the life of your dreams? It may come down to choosing between being unhappy, but having an antique gold pocket watch you wear once every five years, or being happy while wearing a $30 Timex. Valuable antiques and jewelry should be appraised and then sold through a reputable specialized dealer.

If digging through the accumulated dust generates the urge to thin out all your possessions, go with the feeling. Hold a Second Act Tag Sale, the way you would hold a moving sale. Rather than try to run the show yourself, line up a tag sale firm and leave the advertising, pricing, and selling to a pro. You'll end up with more in your pocket, despite paying a fee or commission.

6. *Rent your home.* If you happen to live near a site where people gather every year—close to Augusta National or Churchill Downs, by a campus where parents or alumni gather for graduation or reunions, or near the beach, a lake, or a national park—consider briefly renting your home.

The IRS allows you to collect up to fourteen days rent on a property, tax free. In fact, the income doesn't even need to be reported, and the IRS relies on you or the renter to report longer stays. Rather than trying to do your own marketing, ask for the help of local brokers or organizations—such as the alumni affairs department or the Chamber of Commerce—in exchange for a commission. Simply plan your vacation or visit to a distant relative for the days you'll be renting, making sure your own trip doesn't eat up all your profits. The potential addition to your income or savings depends on the length of time and character of the event. Renting your beach front home for two weeks in July could yield you a tax-free $5,000 annually. Even just a weekend rental of your home for graduation at an Ivy League university could bring in $500 for your transition reserve.

7. *Boost your unearned income.* Have you saved up a nice nest egg over the years? Maybe you have spent years conservatively investing your money in index funds or

government bonds. Perhaps you've concentrated on buying growth stocks and funds for your portfolio. By reallocating your investments to income-generating funds and stocks it's possible to dramatically boost your unearned income.

Obviously, the size of the income you can produce will depend on how much you can invest, and on how much risk you're willing to assume. Unless you've a great deal of money set aside *or* you're a gambler with nerves of steel, it's unlikely you'll be able to live on the income your investments generate. Still, by shifting the bulk of your portfolio from, let's say, growth stocks to dividend producing stocks, you might be able to add enough to your annual income to keep you from having to get a part-time job or sell Grandma's diamonds.

8. *Convert assets to streams of income.* Another way to boost your unearned income is to convert assets into streams of income. Conversion will generate more money for you, and is, I believe, less risky in the long run than reallocating assets. However, it has it's downsides. Let me explain.

You can turn savings into an income stream by selling your securities and using the money to buy annuities. An annuity is simply a contract that guarantees a lifelong income. Generally they're sold by insurance companies, but these days charities and even corporations are getting into the act. While there are many variations and permutations, annuities have some distinct advantages:

- They provide a lifetime income. While you can outlive the income from every other investment, no matter how conservative, it's impossible to outlive an annuity. I sometimes call annuities longevity insurance policies.

- They provide a guaranteed income. It doesn't matter if the market is up or down; if an annuity contractually provides 8 percent interest it will do just that, forever.

- The income is partly tax free. Annuity pay outs are partly comprised of the money you originally paid in. This portion of the reimbursement is tax free. The older you are when you buy an annuity, the larger the portion of your payment that's tax free.

I've become quite the fan of annuities in recent years. I'm a believer in a philosophy of personal finance I described in my book *Die Broke*,[25] which advocates using all your financial resources up while your alive, rather than leaving behind an estate. Annuities are one of the tools that make this approach possible. That being said, there are some disadvantages to annuities. First, they're by and large irrevocable. Once you hand over your money, you can't get it back except in periodic payments. Second, they're subject to inflationary risk. What appears to be a great return in 2003 might not seem so great in 2010. And third, they can be struck by insolvency. Since they're not backed by the government, your return is only as secure as the health of the issuing insurer.

The downsides can be mitigated, however. Irrevocability won't be an issue if you've adequate home, auto, disability, liability, health, and perhaps long-term care insurance. Possible emergencies will then already be covered. You can temper the inflation risk by buying a series of annuities over a period of time, rather than buying one

---

[25] HarperCollins, 1997

large one. By researching the financial health of insurers and buying from a number of those which get the highest grade, you'll minimize any risk of insolvency.

Your savings aren't the only assets you can convert to a stream of income. By taking out a reverse mortgage you can actually get paid a tax-free income to live in your own home.

In a reverse mortgage, a lender agrees to provide a home-owner with a loan using the house as collateral. The amount of the loan is based on the borrower's age, the value of the house, and the prevailing interest rates. Because payments are tied to age, reverse mortgages are most useful to people sixty-five and older. The term of the loan can be for a defined number of years or until the borrower's death. When the loan comes due it has to be paid off either by the borrower or his or her estate. While it's not required, they're almost always paid off by the proceeds of the sale of the house. Payments are tax free since they're technically loan proceeds, not income. They can be made in a lump sum, monthly installments, a line of credit, or any combination.

If you take your money in lifelong monthly payments, and live longer than the actuaries predict, you actually can collect more than the value of your home. If that happens, it's the lender that takes the hit, not the estate. To some-what protect themselves from this happening, lenders will typically only lend 75 percent of the home's value.

The only real downsides to reverse mortgage are that borrowers often must pay closing costs and fees up front, and that interest charges can be high. Although the interest isn't due until the loan is paid off, if a borrower dies soon after taking out the loan the bill could be quite large.

I'm the first to admit reverse mortgages aren't perfect. But for people 65 or older, who have a great deal of wealth tied up in their homes, and who need streams of income for their Second Acts, they can be useful tools.

Exercise 3

Turn to a fresh page in your Second Act notebook and title it INCOME INCREASES. List each of the previously discussed techniques that you're considering implementing and note how much additional income could be generated. Put down conservative estimates. Categorize each income increase either as a one-time boost for your transition reserve, a regular monthly increase, or an irregular increase. In the case of irregular increases, divide the total by 12 so you can express it as a monthly figure. Apply the new income to your deficits and determine whether you've eliminated them entirely, or if not, how much they've been reduced. If you're still short of funds, or would like to boost your safety net, continue on to the next exercise.

HOW CAN I CUT EXPENSES?

I'm always amazed how advice on saving money quickly devolves into talk of clipping coupons and hanging your clothes on a line outside rather that using an electric dryer. Don't get me wrong: those kinds of frugal tips do work. After all, that's why they're part of the traditional litany of budgeting advice offered by most financial advisors. However, I think this conventional approach to saving money has two big drawbacks. First, it focuses on saving you pennies rather than dollars. And second, it requires the sacrifice of convenience, luxury, or pleasure.

Sure, I know the old saying, "watch your pennies and the dollars will take care of themselves." But I believe Groucho Marx had it right when he said, "I realize it's a penny here and a penny there, but look at me: I've worked myself up from nothing to a state of extreme poverty." I think focusing on pennies is a waste of time and effort. You can diligently strive to count your pennies each month and end up with extra money that won't even fill your car with gas. Focus on dollars instead. In fact, focus on hundreds of dollars instead. My adage is: Focus on the $100s, and the pennies won't matter.

You don't need to feel pain in order to save money. You wouldn't know that if you look at most of the common money saving advice. It's as if it was devised by a Puritan minister from old Salem, convinced the only way to drive the demon of extravagance from our bodies is to give us forty lashes. There's a reason people will pay more to go to a movie rather than rent a video tape: It's a better sensory experience. There's a reason people will pay a service charge at a nearby ATM: It will save them time. And there's a reason people will pay for someone else to mow their lawn: They don't like mowing their lawn. It's human nature to prefer pleasure to pain and look for the path of least resistance. Asking people to go against these tendencies only sets them up for failure.

If there weren't painless, big picture savings to be had, I'd be the first to hop on the bulk-buying, brown-bagging band wagon. But there are quite a few ways for you to save considerable sums of money without making sacrifices. Here are some I recommend.

1. *Refinance your mortgage.* I'm sure you know you can save quite a bit of money by refinancing your mortgage to a lower interest rate. Savings of $1,000 annually are not unusual. What you may not know is many lenders now offer deals with no up-front points or fees. That may make shifting worthwhile, even if you'd be dropping just one percent. It literally pays to do the math.

   There are lots of online refinance calculators, but my favorite is at the Quicken.com site (http://www.quicken.com).

2. *Transform your consumer debt.* There's no reason why your efforts to take advantage of lower interest rates must stop with your mortgage loan. If you maintain credit card balances you're likely paying far more in debt service each year than you need.

Take a look at sites like LowCards.com (http://www.lowcards.com) where you can find thoroughly researched lists of low interest, no annual fee credit cards. Go back to Quicken.com, and you can use one of their debt consolidation calculators to determine how much you'd save by shifting your balance from one card to another.

Another option is to take out a home equity loan and use the proceeds to pay off high interest debt. Not only will you end up saving money thanks to the lower rates, but you'll also save money on your taxes since home equity interest payments, unlike other consumer debt, are deductible. Once again, check out the calculators at Quicken.com for exactly how much you could save.

3. *Relocate to lower your cost of living.* Do you need to stay in your current home or community in order to launch your Second Act? If not, and you're in need of money to raise the curtain on your new life, think of moving to a less expensive home in your area or a different area where the cost of living is lower. The savings can be substantial. It's not just the potential of selling real estate for a higher price than it cost you to buy a replacement, either. Living in a smaller home or different area can cut your utility costs, insurance rates, tax bills, clothing bills, and food bills. Moving to a different location could eliminate your money obstacle all together.

For specifics on moving to a less expensive home within your current area, contact a local real estate agent, explain your interests, and ask for some sample listings. Eager at the possibility of earning two commissions (by selling your house and helping you buy another), he or she will bend over backwards being helpful.

For info on relocating, turn back to the Internet. There are many sites that offer cost of living comparisons. My preference is the Relo.com site (http://www.relo.com/home) because it not only provides a cost of living calculator, but also lets you compare info on crime, schools, demographics, and other community factors.

4. *Lease your car.* Why pay more to buy an asset that dramatically depreciates in value than you could to lease the same item? It doesn't make sense. Buy a $20,000 car and you'll not only need to pay, say, $450 a month for a loan, but you could also need to put $2,000 down. Lease the same car and you can pay hundreds less *each month*. Choose to roll the dealer fees and taxes into the lease, and you won't need to put a penny down before walking out with the keys to a brand new vehicle. That will give you thousands of dollars more for your transition reserve.

The downside to leasing is that, unless you buy the car when the lease term expires (generally not a great deal), you'll need to make an auto payment for as long as you have a car. But you'll also always be driving a car that's three years old or less. Not only is that aesthetically pleasing, it also means you'll always be driving a car that's under warranty. Add the lower monthly payments, the lack of a down payment, and the potential for savings on repairs, and I think it's a no-brainer if you want to save money.

5. *Trim your homeowners coverage.* You need insurance for a catastrophe, not a broken window. Increase the deductible on your homeowner's policy from, say, $200 to $2,000,

and you'll maintain your level of coverage while cutting your premiums by $100 or more a year. Dead bolt locks, smoke detectors, and alarm systems will trim the bill even more, generally paying for themselves in three years. Cancel any special riders on valuables, such as jewelry, and put them in a safe deposit box instead. Ask your broker for other suggestions to get the same coverage for less money, and request he or she check around for lower rates with other insurers.

6. *Trim your auto insurance coverage.* You can do the same kind of cost cutting with your auto insurance policy. Eliminate collision coverage for any vehicles more than four years old—it doesn't make sense. Increase your deductibles to at least $1,000 since today even a dent from a shopping cart costs at least that much to repair. Make sure you're not paying for duplicate coverage. For instance, many auto policies have medical coverage that simply replicates your health insurance coverage.

   Before you shop for a new car to lease, check with your broker to see which models cost the least to insure. Generally these are the cars least likely to be stolen. Take a defensive driver class to trim your premium. And make sure your insurer knows your teenage son is attending a college 300 miles away from the car. See whether you can save money by getting your auto coverage from the same insurer that covers your home.

7. *Trim your life insurance coverage.* Whether due to ego or aggressive selling, most people have far more life insurance than they need. You can't put a value on your life, so don't try. Instead, make sure you have enough life insurance to replace your income for three years, giving your dependents time to adjust their lifestyles to your absence.

If you have any outstanding obligations—say your child's college tuition—cover that as well. But that's it. There's no reason to buy enough of a benefit to pay off a mortgage or to try to maintain your family's lifestyle in perpetuity.

Steer clear of whole or universal life policies.[26] They're not only bad investments but they're bad insurance too. Stick with guaranteed annually renewable term coverage. Yes, the rates will go up as you get older. But your needs for insurance should drop as you age, as your savings increase and your obligations decrease. When you have enough set aside on your own, you can drop your life coverage all together.

8. *Appeal your property tax assessment.* There's now a whole specialist group of tax certiorari law firms that appeal property tax assessments and then charge fees based on the savings you win. Most ask for a small up front payment of about $100 to cover the costs of research. This is often refundable if you don't win a reduction. The final fee is equal to your first year's savings. It's a no-lose situation: invest $100 and potentially win four-digit tax savings year after year that can be used to finance your Second Act.

9. *Practice aggressive income tax avoidance.* Are you doing everything you can to legally minimize your tax bills? A savvy accountant can save you far more on your tax bill than his or her fee will cost you.

For instance, rather than having your employer over-withhold taxes from your salary, resulting in a refund, a

---

[26] The only caveat to that is if you are a senior and want to have a life insurance benefit pay for your funeral expenses. Because most insurers won't sell term policies to seniors over a certain age, the only choice is a modest whole life policy.

good CPA can help you revise your W-4 form so that cash stays in your pocket, letting you use it for your Second Act or put it into a transition reserve where it could be earning interest.[27]

Similarly, your accountant, working in concert with your attorney, can arrange for payments made in the event of divorce to take the form of alimony, which is tax deductible, rather than child support, which is not.

10. *Seek out cash discounts*. The next time you hire someone to do repair work or renovations, ask whether he or she offers a cash discount. It costs nothing to ask, and all it will require is a quick trip to the bank for you to save up to 10 percent of the cost of a project. Whether or not the income is reported to the IRS is neither your business nor your responsibility.

Exercise 4

Turn to a fresh page in your Second Act notebook and title it EXPENSE REDUCTIONS. List each of the cost-cutting techniques that you're implementing and note how much you're likely to cut your costs. Jot down a conservative estimate. Categorize each saving as either a regular monthly reduction, or an irregular reduction. In the case of irregular reductions, divide the total by 12 so you can express it as a monthly saving. Once again, apply the savings to your deficits and calculate whether you've eliminated them entirely, or if not, how much they've been reduced.

---

[27] The rule of thumb is that for every $500 in refund you receive you can add one dependent. The number of dependents on your W-4 need not match the number you claim on your return.

THE FINAL OPTION: BORROW THE MONEY

If, after going through all the income-increasing and cost-cutting techniques I've suggested in the previous two exercises you still find money is an obstacle to your Second Act, don't despair. You've one more thing you can do: Borrow the money you need.

There's nothing wrong with borrowing money to change your life. You'd borrow money to renovate your home, wouldn't you? Why not your life? No one thinks twice about taking out a college loan. Neither should you second guess a Second Act loan. Even if your planned Second Act isn't guaranteed to generate a higher income, I still believe it's a sound investment. You cannot put a price on quality of life or happiness.

There are three good places to look for the money: a bank; your own savings; and family and friends.

1. *Borrow from a bank*. I think home-equity loans are tailor made for Second Acts. They're easy to get, the interest rates are low, and the interest is most often tax deductible. These days home-equity loans are probably the easiest and most available source of financing available to Americans. That's why they're my suggestion as the first place to go to borrow money for your Second Act.

   The amount of money you can borrow in a home equity loan depends on what your home is worth and how much is left on your original mortgage. Let's say your home is worth $200,000, and the mortgage balance is $100,000. That means you've $100,000 worth of equity in your home. You can usually borrow against up to 70 percent of that equity. In this example that would translate into a $70,000 loan.

   The most important things to look out for in shopping for a home equity loan are the upfront fees and charges. Luckily, many lenders are offering low and even no-fee loan packages. Still, you need to shop around for a loan the same way you did when you got your first mortgage. Call the commercial banks, credit unions, and savings and loans in your area. Get information on their loan products including interest rates. Find out when and how the rates on any variable rate products are adjusted, and whether or not there are caps. Obviously, double check the fees and any requirements to pay points—percentage points of interest that must be paid up front.

If it's an option, consider applying for a home equity line of credit rather than a regular loan. This usually takes the form of either a credit card or checkbook with a credit limit equal to the amount of the loan. You only pay interest on the money you actually borrow. Personally, I think the checkbook option is preferable since it offers less temptation.

2. *Borrow from yourself.* Do you have money saved for retirement? If you've exhausted your other options and are still short of funds for your Second Act, I don't think there's anything wrong with raiding your retirement accounts. Even the government agrees: You're allowed to take early withdrawals from IRAs to pay for your own higher education expenses without incurring any penalty. Take it from me, if you're doing what you love, you'll have no desire to retire anyway.

3. *Borrow from family and friends.* People who love you want you to be happy. That's why they're excellent candidates to help finance your Second Act. But borrowing from them can become sticky, so, unless there's an incredibly wealthy and generous cousin in your family tree, I'd make family and friends the third borrowing option, after home equity loans and tapping your own savings.

Cast a discriminating eye on your friends and relations. The one objection you can't overcome is someone saying they don't have the money. Perhaps you've a sister who earned a great deal of money in the dot com years. Maybe a friend has just sold his business and is swimming in cash. There's nothing wrong with asking for help in making the life of your dreams become real. The key, however, is to present it as a pragmatic venture, because, despite their love, they want to know this is a loan and not a gift.

Set this meeting up at their home, on a weekend or evening, if possible, to subtly reinforce the personal nature of the relationship. At the same time, insist on the tone being that of a semiformal discussion. Come to them with what amounts to a business plan, including the breakdown of your expenses, your projected income, and how long you believe it will take for you to begin paying them back. Show them how you have invested time, effort, and money in the project. Suggest a payment plan with a long term and an interest of around prime. Explain how you'll pay them back if things don't work out as you plan. For instance, by taking out a home equity loan or using your savings, if you haven't already, or by selling your home. Even while describing their safety net, be positive and upbeat. Any doubts you have will become theirs. Make your best case, once. Don't try to counter any objections. . . that will only lead to more discomfort. Whether they agree or refuse, express your undying love and gratitude.

With all the options I've offered for increasing your income, trimming your expenses, and borrowing funds, I think I've given you the tools necessary to overcome any money barriers between you and your Second Act. But you need to be willing to take charge. You must decide whether your Second Act is worth going into your boss and asking for raise; or worth working through your insurance coverage; or worth taking out a home equity loan; or, even though I don't think it will be necessary, worth bringing your lunch to work in a brown paper bag. Opening the money door really is a matter of choice. If you truly want to lead the life of your dreams, money is no obstacle.

CHAPTER 7

Duration:
Helping Hands
and Shortcuts

*"What Romantic terminology called genius or talent or inspiration is
nothing other than finding the right road empirically, following one's
nose, taking shortcuts."*

—ITALO CALVINO

Today, instant gratification isn't fast enough. We're used to getting our glasses made while we wait, our photos developed and printed in an hour, and our packages delivered overnight to anywhere in the world. We pay at the pump, use drive-through windows, and put transmitters on our cars so we don't need to stop at toll booths. It's no wonder, then, that so many people worry about how long it will take them to achieve a Second Act.

That's particularly true for people whose Second Act takes them in an entirely new direction. After all, if you've been an accountant for ten years and are planning to become a pastry chef, it appears as if you need to go back to square one. And that would seem to mean you'll need at least another ten years, if not more, just to get to the level in your new field that you've already achieved on your current path. Any additional schooling or training just makes the time needed appear even more daunting. But there are a couple of things you're probably not factoring into your time estimates.

IT NEVER TAKES AS LONG AS YOU THINK

To begin with, there are ways to streamline every process. (I'll be offering some general suggestions in the second part of this chapter, which you can then apply to your specific Second Act.) And besides, no matter how different your first act is from your second, you don't need to start from square one.

In the years you've spent on your current path you've learned far more than just some specialized jargon and skills. You've learned how to listen and how to get along with others. You've learned when to be diplomatic and when to be candid. You've learned to pick your battles; when it's important to compromise and when it's important to make a stand. You've learned how to spot people you can trust and people you can't. You're more mature and wise today then you were when you started your first act. That maturity and wisdom will speed up your Second Act. It's like the difference between a first trip to a foreign country and a second.

The first time you travel to an exotic city you don't know what to expect. Sure, you've read guidebooks, but that's no replacement for actually being there—just as studying an occupation in school is no replacement for actually practicing it. On your first trip you pack everything you think you'll need. By your second trip you pack lighter, knowing you won't need certain things and where you can, if need be, find the things you've left behind. On your first trip you're overscheduled and tense about getting everything done. By your second trip you've learned what you like to do and are more relaxed about the experience. On your first trip you spend lots of time and money. By the second you use your resources much more efficiently.

Believe me: Your Second Act will not take as long as you think. I'm not saying it will happen overnight. I'm just saying it's probably not going to be the long ordeal you fear. It certainly won't take you just as long to get as far as in your first act. Before I offer some techniques for accelerating the process even more, let's make sure duration really is an obstacle.

Do you know for sure how long it is likely to take, or are you just assuming it will be a time-consuming process? If you don't know for sure, duration is an internal barrier for you. Tackle the first exercise to do some due diligence and get your facts. If you're sure about how long your Second Act will take, you can move on to the second exercise for ways of trimming the time involved. But before you jump ahead I'd like to make a pitch for you to start with the first exercise anyway. The added certainty of double checking your estimates can be reassuring. And, some elements of the first exercise will give you a leg up on the second. The choice, however, is yours.

HOW LONG WILL IT TAKE?

If you don't know for sure how long your Second Act will take, you need to find someone who does. Who knows best how long your dream will take to achieve? Someone who has successfully done whatever it is you want to do. Start reaching out to others for guidance, advice, and wisdom. Who you reach out to, and how you contact them, depends on your Second Act.

If your dream doesn't involve a competitive field it will be easy to find willing mentors. For instance, if you're looking to become a parent you'll be able to turn to friends and family for advice, or for referrals to obstetricians, child care businesses, and support groups. In noncompetitive areas people are more than willing to provide all the information you'd like. Actually, you'll probably get so much advice you'll be tired of hearing opinions.

Famous Second Act

HILLARY RODHAM CLINTON

In 1991, before the world had heard much about her husband, Hillary Rodham Clinton had already been named one of the 100 most powerful lawyers in America by the National Law Journal. Her role as an adviser to her husband, President Bill Clinton, coupled with her very public defense of him, both during his initial run for president and later when he was impeached, made her a political lightning rod. But rather than retreating from public view or simply "standing by her man," Clinton launched a Second Act by running for the U.S. Senate from her adopted state of New York. On November 7, 2000, Hillary Rodham Clinton had the most dramatic Second Act of any first lady by becoming Senator Clinton. ■

On the other hand, if your dream is success in a competitive field you might find people hesitant to offer help. Personally, I've never understood this kind of reticence to lend a helping hand. Success in even the most competitive fields isn't a zero sum game. Another's victory isn't necessarily your loss. I believe that what goes around comes around and that you can't hope to maintain your success unless you help others: To keep it, you must be willing to give it away. Unfortunately, not everyone shares my view. There are many small business owners, for example, who are loathe to help others start their own small businesses. Successful artists and writers are infamous for refusing to give practical advice and counsel to wannabes. How can you get around this hesitation and gain the wise mentoring you need to figure out how long your Second Act will take? I have two suggestions:

1. *Expand your mentor search.* People outside your geographic area or specialty will be less reticent to become mentors. If, for instance, your dream is to open a specialty camera shop in your hometown, you might find camera store owners in the immediate area reticent to do anything other than discourage you. That's because they may see you as a direct threat to their livelihood. Rather than try to convince them otherwise, seek out camera store owners from towns outside your area and ask them for help. Let's say you want to be a freelance travel writer. Other travel writers may be less than forthcoming, seeing you as a competitor for assignments. Instead, look for guidance from writers who specialize in different areas, say business or technology. These mentors from slightly outside your area can provide you with solid general advice, which you then can supplement with more specific information you gather from seminars, organizations, associations, or government agencies.

2. *Target the most successful and experienced.* I believe people tend to aim too low when looking for mentors in competitive fields. They think the CEO and the famous architect are too busy and important to be bothered with questions from people interested in entering their fields. Instead, they target lower level executives and less well known professionals, believing they'll be more likely to spare the time for a newbie. Actually, the reverse is true. The more successful and experienced someone is, the less likely they'll feel threatened by your approach and the more likely they'll have a sense of gratitude they'd like to repay by helping others. This is particularly true for someone who has succeeded in a Second Act of his/her own.

Famous Second Act

SHERWOOD ANDERSON

In 1900, after an early life of erratic schooling, odd jobs, and service in the Spanish American War, twenty-four-year-old Sherwood Berton Anderson took a job as an advertising copywriter in his native Ohio. He married, started his own mail order business in Cleveland which failed, and then became manager of a paint factory. In 1912 he had an emotional and mental breakdown, walked out on his family and quit his job, blaming the conflicting demands of family, business, and creativity. He renounced his "bourgeois lifestyle," left his wife, and raised the curtain on his Second Act, moving to Chicago where he took another job in advertising. But he also became part of the "Chicago Group," an informal circle of writers, including Theodore Dreiser and Carl Sandburg. With their help he began publishing. His third novel, *Winesburg, Ohio,* received critical acclaim. He continued writing with mixed commercial and critical success. He traveled extensively, sharing an apartment with William Faulkner for a time, but finally settling in Marion, Virginia, where he bought and edited both of the local weekly newspapers (one Republican, one Democrat). He died in 1941 while on a goodwill lecture tour of South America. ∎

In my experience it's no more difficult getting to meet with someone very successful or well known than it is with anyone else. No man or woman is an island. You can always find or create connections if you're resourceful. I've helped clients make connections with well-known individuals through sources at professional associations, pastors, house painters, masseuses, and one time, a bookie.

Don't hesitate to turn to articles or books about successful individuals for ideas and insights. But here to, I'd suggest steering toward works by and about more seasoned individuals. The memoir of a seventy year old will provide you with more useful insights than the autobiography of a forty year old. Take it from me, it's real easy to ignore life's lessons when you're forty. On the other hand, you've got to try really hard not to learn something by the time you're seventy.

Exercise 1

Open your Second Act notebook to a blank page and head it MENTORS. If you're looking for mentors in a noncompetitive area, work your way through your address book. Go through family members first, noting any whose experiences could be applicable. Move on to friends next. Finally, turn to acquaintances, coworkers, and professional contacts. If you're looking for mentors in competitive areas, go the library and do some research in the reference room. For sources outside your geographic area, look through telephone directories of surrounding communities. For mentors outside your specialty, look through the membership lists of professional associations or trade groups. For well-known and successful sources, consult magazine and newspaper indices and use Internet search engines. Write each name you come up with on it's own line, about one-half inch from the left hand edge of the page.

Once you've found willing mentors, ask for their educated and experienced estimates on how it will take for your Second Act to succeed. Whether it's your cousin who had a child at forty-two using donated eggs or the CEO of a chain of camera stores, encourage them to be as conservative as possible. I'd rather you end up surprised at how quickly it happened rather than disappointed in how long it took. Do your best to develop relationships with all your sources and maintain them. You'll be coming back to your mentors and advisors again in the next exercise.

Write what each has say in the space next to his or her name. Before you leave each mentor, ask for suggestions of others you should speak with. If any sound like good fits, add those names to your list, contact them, and go through the process again. There's no such thing as too much good advice.

Bear in mind that the more closely someone's experience parallels your own, the more accurate their estimate will be. For example, if you're a forty-one-year-old woman trying to have a biological child for the first time, the estimate you get from your thirty-nine-year-old friend who went to the fertility specialist is probably more applicable than the information you get from your twenty-five-year-old cousin who just had her second baby. Similarly, if you're opening a camera shop the advice you get from the woman who opened a successful photo shop in a nearby city is more valuable than the guidance of a man who started a sporting goods store in your town. Go through your list and, to the left of each name, place three stars (***) next to those whose experience most closely matches your own Second Act, two stars (**) next to the names of those who experiences are somewhat near yours, and one star (*) next to the names of those whose experiences are only tangentially related.

Of course, listen to everyone and factor everything into your decision making. Remember that your maturity and the resulting willingness to listen, is a big part of speeding up your Second Act.

Weighing your three star sources heaviest and your one star sources the least, come up with your own estimate of how long it will take for you to reach the life of your dreams. How does that fit in with your earlier assumptions? Perhaps you overestimated the time it would require. Or, maybe you didn't realize all that could be involved. In either case, factor this newly confirmed duration estimate into your calculations. Do you have enough money saved to finance a transition of this length? Consider whether your spouse or family could cope with this long a process. Finally, ask yourself whether, at your age, this kind of Second Act makes sense. For instance, while it's possible for a seventy year old to go to law school, pass the bar, and start his or her practice, does it make sense?

Between you and me, I think it does. When you're doing what you love, the process of becoming is as joyous as the act of being. If you've always wanted to be a lawyer, studying law will be a pleasure, not a grind. Besides, I know there are ways you can speed the works.

If you discover that duration is indeed an obstacle, move on to Exercise 2. However, if you now know duration isn't going to be an obstacle you have two choices: you can skip the rest of this chapter and move on to the next item on your CLOSED DOOR list; or you can go through the next exercise anyway, in an effort to trim the time involved. I'd suggest you go through Exercise 2 even if duration isn't the obstacle you supposed. Even though the process may be something you'll enjoy, I still think it makes sense to get to your goal as soon as possible.

SPEEDING THE PROCESS

There's nothing wrong with cutting corners or taking short cuts on the path to your Second Act. I'm not suggesting you endanger yourself or others by flying an aircraft without training, or practicing medicine without a license. I'm just saying there's no reason why you shouldn't do everything you can to legitimately speed the process. In my experience there are four general techniques for shortening the time required for a Second Act: replacing requirements; using mentors; leveraging someone else's power; and studying for the test. Using as many of these as you possibly can will maximize the amount of time you can trim from the process.

1. *Replace requirements.* The list of requirements for many fields isn't drawn up with Second Acts in mind. Often it's prepared with an eye toward training young, inexperienced, and perhaps immature individuals. As a result it often involves some very general requirements that serve as a foundation for some very specialized needs. Quite often, people launching a Second Act will have training and experience from their first act that can substitute for most of the general, and even some of the specific requirements of their new path.

   The most obvious example is getting academic credit for life experience. When I went back to college to get my bachelor's degree, I was able to cut the required classes in half by preparing reports and memos that demonstrated how my life experience could compensate for some classes in finance, management, marketing, and communications. One way to maximize the use to which you can put your past experience is to find someone on the inside to help you out. . . like a mentor.

2. *Get a mentor.* Using a mentor was a large part of determining whether or not duration was actually an obstacle to your Second Act. Mentors are also extremely helpful in shortening the process. Not only can they advise you about how to spin your experiences so they can be used to replace requirements, but they can also point out shortcuts peculiar to your particular situation. For instance, a long-time teacher in a particular school district could give you tips on how best to package yourself as a candidate for

jobs in that district. If you were successful in finding a well-known or powerful mentor back in Exercise 1 that will help in the next technique to accelerate the process.

3. *Leverage someone else's power.* For better or worse, there are individuals in every field who have the power and influence to eliminate or mitigate red tape and requirements. The individual who donated millions of dollars to a university is apt to be able to get admission for a favored candidate. Someone who is a major client of a company is likely to be able to make a powerful recommendation.

Such influence isn't limited to the worlds of business and education. A well-known physician could help you get in to see a renowned fertility specialist who otherwise isn't taking new clients. A theater owner can get you a face-to-face meeting with a casting director. A successful author can get you a lunch meeting with a magazine editor.

Using connections to get ahead is a fact of life in almost every realm of life. There's no reason why you shouldn't try to take advantage. Leveraging someone else's power is also nothing to be embarrassed about and no indication of how successful you'll be at your chosen Second Act. Harry S Truman was a bankrupt small businessman when he used the influence of a local political boss to get named a judge. That didn't detract from the success of his Second Act.

4. *Study for the test.* Some fields require candidates to pass an exam to receive the credential or license needed to practice. Traditionally, people only take the exam after years of study in the field. For instance, people usually take the CPA exam after studying accounting for four years. Often, there's no actual requirement for getting this prior education; it's just an accepted norm. If you're launching a

Second Act I don't believe you need to accept norms that stand in your way. After all, if you accepted the conventional wisdom you wouldn't be pursuing a Second Act.

There are hundreds of services and resources designed to help people specifically pass these credentializing exams. There are books on how to take civil service exams. There are classes on how to take the Law School Aptitude Test and other standardized tests. There are Web sites that offer complete syllabi and sample exams for taking any number of professional certification tests. Almost none of these preparatory programs requires anything other than the ability to pay. You can dramatically cut the duration of a process by just devoting yourself to passing the exam, rather than going through the entire traditional process.

In some fields all you need is an exam to claim the credential. For instance, to be a certified archivist all you need is to pass an exam given by the professional association. Having done that, you can often fulfill any remaining requirements through on-the-job training or past experience. To get your CPA license in some states, for example, you'd need to work as an accountant for a period of time as well as passing the exam.

Once again there's nothing wrong with focusing on the test to speed the process. You are not the traditional candidate so there's no reason you should have to force yourself into the traditional process. The wisdom and experience you bring from your first act more than compensates for any course work you're skipping. There's also no shame in cutting corners this way. Abraham Lincoln "read law" rather than going to law school, and he turned out to be a pretty good attorney.

Famous Second Act

HARRY S TRUMAN

Having farmed his family's land near Independence, Missouri, from more than twelve years, thirty-three-year-old Harry S Truman decided to enlist in the Army when the nation entered World War II. Truman rose to the rank of captain. Returning from the war, but not wanting to return to farming, Truman joined a friend in opening a clothing store. It went bankrupt. Encouraged by local Democratic boss Tom Prendergast, Truman ran for and won a position as county judge in 1922 and began his Second Act. He continued as a judge until 1934 when, as a supporter of Franklin Delano Roosevelt's "New

---

Exercise 2

Take out your Second Act notebook. Turn to a blank page and title it REPLACING REQUIREMENTS. Divide the page into two columns. In the lefthand column, list all the requirements for your chosen Second Act. Refer back to the notes from all your earlier meetings and discussions. Leaf back to the information you pulled off the Internet from the Bureau of Labor Statistics web site. Take a look at the help wanted ads in trade journals or consumer publications. Now, in the righthand column, note anything from your own past that could serve as a replacement for these requirements.

Let's say that after ten years as a magazine writer, you want to become an English teacher at a private school. You discover that most of the positions seem to require a masters degree in the subject you're planning to teach, a certain number of credits of a foreign

Deal," he ran for the U.S. Senate. Elected, and then re-elected in 1940, Truman came to national attention by chairing a Senate committee investigating corruption in defense contracting. When FDR was nominated for an unprecedented fourth term in June 1944, Truman was picked as his running mate. After only eighty-two days as Vice President, Truman was thrust into the presidency by FDR's death. Known for his "plain speaking," Truman was in the White House for the tumultuous end of World War II and the beginning of the Cold War. He won re-election in 1948 in America's most famous upset victory. The one-time failed retailer is now one of America's most admired Presidents. ■

language, and some pedagogical experience. In the lefthand column of the page you write down: Masters in English, foreign language credits, and teaching experience. Without pursuing shortcuts you might need to go back to school for two years for a masters degree, as well as two or three classes in a foreign language, and classes in teaching or educational theory. But while you don't formally meet these requirements you can offer some excellent replacements that can dramatically reduce the time it would take to launch your Second Act.

Instead of a masters degree in English, you've been a successful journalist and author for ten years. You may not have any college credits in a foreign language, but you were on assignment in France for two years. You may not be classically fluent, but you were able to converse without trouble. Finally, although you've never previously taught English to youngsters you've taught creative writing to adults, have been a guest lecturer at colleges and conferences, and have coached little league baseball for six years. So, in the right column, opposite Masters in English you write: ten years as professional journalist and author. Next to foreign language credits you note: conversational French and two years residency. Finally, to the right of teaching experience you can note: adult education, college and conference lecturing, and little league coaching.

Turn back to the page in your Second Act notebook that lists all your mentors. Contact them all again, this time in order to get their advice on ways you can shorten the process. In addition, determine whether any of your mentors have any power that you could use to your advantage. If they don't have power you can leverage, ask whether they have any contacts or connections with powerful individuals who could help you cut corners. Add the names of any such people to your mentor list.

Finally, head a fresh page in your notebook STUDY AIDS. Consult the research sources you've found most fruitful in the past for any leads on classes, courses, or publications that offer to train you to take licensing or credentializing exams. Gather all the contact information for each study aid and find out the cost of each and how much time is involved. Note how much time each study aid could potentially trim from the process.

It's difficult to determine ahead of time exactly how much time you'll save by using each of these techniques. In situations where you're able to find replacements for all your new requirements and can enlist the help of a powerful individual, you may be able to trim the time you'll need to invest dramatically. In other situations you may be able to cut the process down to just taking a class designed to help you pass a test. Of course, there are some situations that simply can't be sped up. For example, if you want to give birth to a child it's going to take at least nine months, no matter how many powerful people you enlist on your side. Seriously though, try not to get upset if you can't achieve instant gratification. Your goal should be to make the time required manageable, not to make it disappear entirely. Give yourself a chance to enjoy the process. You've every right to pause, if not stop, to savor a cup of coffee. You're on the path to the life of your dreams, so the scenery will be thrilling.

CHAPTER 8

Physical Condition: Just Do It

"Talent counts thirty percent; appearance counts seventy."

—CHINESE PROVERB

I'm not a psychotherapist. Still, because of the holistic nature of my life coaching practice, I do get into a lot of areas that most career, financial, and legal advisors tend to ignore. I talk with people about parenting, marriage, and lifestyle as much as I do about salary, investing, and real estate. I don't believe I can accurately help you make sound career decisions, for instance, without helping you factor in all the personal elements that are, or may be, affected by those decisions.

My job, as a life coach and an author, is to help you achieve your goals, whatever they may be. As you can tell from reading this book, a large part of what I do involves refining these goals and developing workable strategies to succeed. My role isn't to help you figure out why you feel the way you do or why you have a particular goal. My job is simply to help ensure you get to where you want to go as quickly and efficiently as possible.

So when you list physical condition as either an internal or external barrier to your Second Act, I don't approach it as an invitation for analysis. Instead, I approach it as a concrete specific obstacle we need to overcome. (You'll find I treat other "psychological obstacles" similarly.) I don't discourage talk therapy. In fact, if prompted, I'll recommend a therapist with whom I've worked in the past. It's just that I see psychotherapy as a separate, more long-term process than the one on which I'm working. Spend as much time talking to a therapist as you'd like. Just don't let it interfere with the practical steps you need to take to launch your Second Act.

INTERNAL OR EXTERNAL— IT'S ALL THE SAME

Do you think you're too short, or your nose is too big, or you don't have enough hair, or you weigh too much? If a certain physical condition *isn't* required for your Second Act, yet you're afraid your own physical condition will be an obstacle, you have a body image problem. If a certain physical condition *is* required for your Second Act, and you don't measure up, you have a body problem. In this case, it doesn't really matter whether the obstacle is in your head or out in the world; The ways to address it are all the same.

Volumes have been written on the causes of poor body image and how to overcome this malady. Those books have been written with the goal of getting people to overcome their mistaken perceptions and develop a healthy self image. That's not the goal of this book. To be blunt, all I'm concerned with is getting you to raise the curtain on your Second Act. That's why my advice is the same whether your physical barrier is internal or external: Fix it. Do whatever it takes externally to at least temporarily make you feel good enough about yourself to launch your Second Act.

Sure, this may seem like superficial advice. But you know what? I've seen it work wonders. I've worked with many people

---

Famous Second Act

MICHAEL J. FOX

Michael J. Fox, after early success as a child actor in Canada, moved to Los Angeles to further his career. He landed a role in a television series called *Family Ties,* and his charm and humor made him a fixture on American television screens for seven years. His success soon stretched to film, notably in the *Back to the Future* series of films in 1985, 1989, and 1990. Broadening his range, Fox took dramatic roles, including that of a young idealistic presidential aide in 1995's *The American President.* He returned to prime time television again, the next year, starring in *Spin City.* In 1999 Fox announced he is suffering from Parkinson's Disease. One year later he decided to leave *Spin City* and begin his Second Act, concentrating on raising money and awareness for Parkinson's through his Michael J. Fox Foundation for Parkinson's Research. In 2002 his memoir, *Lucky Man*, became an international bestseller. ■

---

who felt bad about their appearance. I've encouraged them to do whatever they needed externally to fix it. Once they've been able to start living the life of their dreams, their attitude toward themselves changes. They start to feel good. They begin to see themselves as people of worth, valuable individuals, worthy of love and respect and admiration. Maybe your physical problem is all in your head. Perhaps it came from some childhood trauma, your parents' own upbringing, or your birth order in the family. I don't know. What I do know is that once you change your life, the poor self image that lies at the heart of your mistaken body image will be improved, and you'll start to see yourself as a beautiful, successful human being.

IS YOUR SECOND ACT A PHYSICAL IMPOSSIBILITY?

Physical condition is the one barrier that potentially could be insurmountable. Certain Second Acts, by their very nature, require specific physical characteristics. Let's say you've dreamed of being a large animal veterinarian ever since you were a young child spending summers on your grandparent's farm. But despite having grown in age, you're not that much larger physically. You simply aren't strong enough to safely work with large animals. You can have all the skill and knowledge in the world, and you still won't be able to work with livestock on your own. Maybe you've dreamed of being a military pilot. If your natural vision isn't good enough, no amount of training is going to get you into a military cockpit. In some professions, no amount of desire can compensate for a lack of a physical skill. If your dream is to give birth to a child, and you learn that you physically cannot carry a baby to term, there's no way around this barrier. I can help you do a lot, but I can't perform miracles.[28]

On the other hand, some dreams may be very difficult, due to physical obstacles, but aren't necessarily impossible. For example, just because you're overweight, or balding, doesn't mean you

---

[28] I'm not discounting the power of prayer. However, it would be irresponsible—maybe even sacrilegious—of me to suggest that if you pray hard enough your dream will come true. I know first hand that prayer is powerful and helpful, but not in that way. I encourage prayer. But I'd suggest you pray for comfort, for strength, for patience, for acceptance, or for understanding, not for a miracle.

can't get a job as a model. Not only could you change your condition, but alternatively, you could pursue opportunities for "plus size" or "common man" modeling jobs.

It's rare that people have come to me with impossible dreams. I think most people have an innate sense about where to draw the line between what's impossible and what's difficult, but possible. If you've gotten this far in the book with a goal that's a physical impossibility, it means one of three things. Perhaps you don't really want to succeed at your Second Act, and, as a result, have chosen a goal you know can't be reached. Maybe you're in deep denial about your own physical limitations. Or, it could be you really haven't done a good job of getting past youthful fantasizing and distilling your dream to its essential elements.

If you don't think you deserve to lead the life of your dreams, or can't accept that some things are beyond your physical abilities, I'd suggest you set this book aside and contact a psychotherapist. Spend the time required to work these things out, and then come back to this book to start your Second Act all over again. I'll be here waiting for you. Don't worry about timing. As I'll explain in another chapter, while there may be better times to launch a Second Act, there's never a bad time to turn your life around.

If you find yourself facing a physical barrier that's impossible to overcome, and you realize you simply haven't done a good job of distilling your dream, the solution is to return to that project.

Exercise 1

Pick a time when you can sit and think for a couple of hours without being disturbed. Make yourself a cup of tea or coffee. Find a nice comfortable chair. Take out your Second Act notebook. Turn back to the pages titled PASSIONS, STRENGTHS & WEAKNESSES, and NEEDS. Read through those lists again, thinking

Famous Second Act

HEATHER MILLS

In 1977, at the age of nine, Heather Mills was left to care for her younger siblings after her mother abandoned the family to flee her abusive husband. Fleeing the abuse herself, Heather ran away in 1981 and lived on the street for four months. She found odd jobs, started two small businesses, and eventually ended up modeling. In 1990, at age twenty-two, she went on holiday to Slovenia, fell in love with the area, and decided to start a new life there as a ski instructor. During her stay, the Yugoslavian civil war broke out. In an effort to help her friends, many of whom had become refugees, Mills launched a Second Act. She started a refugee crisis center. Mills commuted between Slovenia, Austria, and the United Kingdom, doing modeling work to raise money for refugees. On one such trip back to the U.K., she was in an auto accident that resulted in serious internal injuries as well as the loss of her left leg below the knee. Realizing her modeling career might be at an end, she decided to sell her story to the press. Mills began speaking and lecturing on charitable causes and issues. She continued modeling as well. In 2002 she married Sir Paul McCartney. ■

about what you've written. Try to look at them with an open mind. After giving them some thought, turn to a blank page and write down what you now perceive your dream to be. Try focusing it as sharply as you can by very clearly defining your terms and probing possible options.

Let's say your dream is to give birth to a child. Does that mean you want to experience the physical birthing process? Maybe it means you want to be a mother, which doesn't require you to give birth or to have an infant. Maybe you should consider using a surrogate mother. Perhaps you could investigate other artificial means of reproduction. How do you feel about adoption?

The idea is to ask yourself and answer the kind of questions that will help make your dream more achievable. The more options you're willing to pursue, the easier parenthood becomes. If your goal is actually to become a parent, not just to give birth, then physical barriers don't matter.

Rewrite your dream on a fresh page in your notebook. Edit down the language as much as you can, trimming it to as few words as possible. Now, go back to Chapter 4 and start analyzing what, if anything, still stands in the way of your newly refined dream.

IF SOMETHING NEEDS TO BE CHANGED, CHANGE IT.

What is the physical barrier you think, or know, you'll be confronting in your difficult, but not impossible Second Act? Maybe you want to be a firefighter but aren't in good enough shape physically to pass the exam. Perhaps you're interested in pursuing a career in broadcast journalism, but you have a tendency to blush. Or, it could be you want to teach, but have a stuttering problem. Whatever physical obstacle you're confronting, odds are good there's a solution at hand.

If you're overweight, and believe or know it will be problematic, join Weight Watchers and a health club. Go to Jenny Craig and take up jogging. Start the Atkins diet and hire a personal trainer. If the problem is more severe, or these techniques haven't worked for you in the past, investigate liposuction and stomach stapling. Need to be in better shape? Start lifting weights and exercising religiously.

Is there something about your appearance you think will be distracting and make your Second Act more difficult? Get a nose job. Have your teeth straightened and whitened. Buy Rogaine, have a hair transplant, or buy a toupee. Dye your hair if you think it will help. Think you're too short? Wear heels or buy elevator shoes. Have breast reduction, or enhancement surgery if you think it will help. Feel you look older than your years, and afraid my advice on overcoming age barriers isn't sufficient? Get a face lift. If you have blushing, sweating, or wrinkle problems, investigate Botox injections.

Investigate all your options and pursue them systematically, from least expensive and invasive to most costly and extensive, for as long as it takes for you to find one that works for you.

There's no reason to feel ashamed or embarrassed about such "artificial" alterations in your physical condition or appearance. I think that anything that makes it easier for you to live the life of your dreams, short of committing a felony, isn't just acceptable, it's wonderful.

And as far as the cost and time involved. . . so what. Factor those elements back into your calculations, and, if necessary, use the techniques for overcoming money and duration obstacles I offer in other chapters.

There's no reason to let a poor self image or a bulbous nose keep you from pursuing the life of your dreams. What better reason could there be for self improvement?

Exercise 2

Turn to a fresh page in your Second Act notebook and title it PHYSICAL OBSTACLES. List the specific physical traits you feel you need to either improve, eliminate, or add, in order to achieve your goals.

Banish the idea from your mind that these are flaws. They aren't. We were all made in God's image. These are modifications to your packaging, nothing more. Compiling this list is no different than, say, writing down that you need to wear a suit and tie to a job interview.

If you are a woman, you don't need to ask anyone else for help in this exercise. You are probably your own most severe critic when it comes to your appearance. In fact, it's a good idea to compile this list on a day when you're feeling good about yourself, just to balance out any excessive self criticism. If you feel for some reason that you must get an outside opinion, ask a hair cutter or make up artist about facial features. They'll have the training and experience to spot potential problems, yet won't have a vested interest in the possible corrections. A dressmaker or designer could offer similar advice on possible body issues.

On the other hand, if you're a man, please do ask someone else for help. Most men think they look like Paul Newman even if it's Oliver Hardy staring back at them in the mirror. Don't ask another man; he's as blind to your flaws as his own. Don't ask your mother either. She'll either think you're flawless or hopeless, depending on her personality. Instead, ask your wife, or girl-friend, or sister for objective input.

With your list compiled, note every possible treatments for each trait. Now, do some research, either online or at the library, about how long each of the treatments could take, and what it could cost. For example, if you need to lose 50 pounds, your research might show that by exercising four times a week and following the Weight Watchers plan you could lose up to one pound per week. Some telephone calls would then tell you how much it costs to join Weight Watchers for a year, and what are the fees for an annual health club membership. Do your due diligence on every option you could pursue.

Take your estimate of the cost and time required for each possible treatment, and turn to the chapters on overcoming duration and money obstacles. Add these new factors into the calculations about whether money or the time involved are indeed obstacles.

If you discover that the treatments necessary to overcome physical barriers don't create new problems for you, that's great. Throw out the ice cream and head over to the gym. If, however, your efforts to overcome your physical obstacles will create or increase money or duration barriers, don't worry. You can tackle those as well. If you want your dream so much that you're ready to change your physical characteristics, you've clearly got the determination to overcome anything.

CHAPTER 9

Consent and Support: Asking Is Enough

"Consult. To seek another's approval of a course already decided on."

—AMBROSE BIERCE

I'm always amazed at how people remain hungry for others' approval, no matter their age or level of success. World famous actors have come to me for help with financial projects, and I've found them desperate for validation. Multimillionaire entrepreneurs have sat in my office and talked about how they're still trying to prove themselves. I can relate.

From an early age I was always striving to succeed in order to please my parents. For whatever reason, from the time I could walk they stressed the need for me to achieve. My father used to cut out newspaper articles about successful men and put them on my pillow for me to read before I went to sleep. It was as if he thought I would absorb their success through osmosis. As if looking for the approval of my own parents wasn't enough, I was desperate for my father-in-law's as well. He was a very successful businessman. I harbored the sense that he thought I wasn't good enough for his daughter. I spent nearly half a century looking for validation and approval from my parents and in-laws. So I know how strong that need can be.

But I must tell you, unless you truly need another's consent or support in order for your Second Act to succeed—say you need a spouse to pick up the slack with child care—getting it isn't essential. Sure, it would be nice if everyone you care about, and everyone whose opinion you value, agreed with everything you were doing and was pulling for you to succeed. Unfortunately, human relations aren't that simple or straight forward. People who love you may, either because they honestly disagree with you, or because it fills some psychological need in them, refuse to support your efforts. What you need to realize is something I eventually came to figure out: That while having support would be a plus, not having it isn't a minus.

If you let nonessential consent and support deter you from your Second Act, you've no one to blame but yourself. As Eleanor Roosevelt said, "No one can make you feel inferior without your consent." This is your life, not theirs. Do you want to be happy and live the life of your dreams? If so, you've got to stand up for yourself and go for it. You want to lead your life, the one that resonates deep within you, not the life others think you should lead. There's a famous Buddhist proverb that says, "Better your own dharma (path) badly done, than the dharma of another." Now is a time when society's conventional guidelines and precepts have been tossed aside. If you needlessly replace them with the prejudices and opinions of someone else, rather than pursuing your own hopes and dreams, you'll be losing out on the chance of a lifetime. The choice is yours: Live your life and be happy, or live someone else's life and be unhappy.

That being said, I still think you should ask for consent and support, even if it's not essential, and even if you strongly suspect you won't get it. I know. It will probably be easier not to let any naysayer know what you're planning to do. That way you won't hear their complaints and criticisms and warnings; they won't rain on your parade. But hearing those things, while unpleasant, just might be helpful. Even a broken clock is right twice a day. Maybe somewhere amidst the reflexive negativity and put downs, there will be a germ of truth or a point you'd do well to consider.

Besides, you've nothing to be embarrassed about by going after your dreams. To keep it a secret or to conceal it in any way gives the naysayers more power than they deserve. Keep the truth hidden and, in some way, you're showing you agree with their image of you. Let them know what you're doing, ask for their support or at least understanding, but make it clear that you'll proceed without it, and you're making a powerful statement of your independence and the strength of your commitment.

Sometimes asking for support and consent can be two separate steps in an approval process. Let's say you're tired of your job as a working musician and you'd like to go back to college to become an accountant. At first you may need to ask your spouse simply for his or her support of the general concept; are they okay with your investigating what would be involved. Later, after you've uncovered all the closed doors and figured out ways to open them, you may need his or her consent for, perhaps, picking up more of the child care slack while you're attending class.

In this two-step process you'll almost never be turned down when you ask for support, because there's really no sacrifice required by the other person. Still, it's worth going through the motion because it shows how much respect and concern you have for the other party's feelings. Having won support early on will make it easier to win consent later.

The techniques you use to ask for both consent and support are the same whether or not it's crucial to the success of your Second Act, or it's a one- or two-step process. The only difference is that in cases when consent and support aren't essential you don't need to persevere until you succeed; you can stop once you feel you've made your case.

FIND OUT THE PRICE
OF CONSENT. . . AND PAY IT

Getting someone's consent and support is a process, not just a one-hour project. That's why it's important to make your approach as early along your own path to a Second Act as you can. The sooner you ask someone for their consent and support, the more flattering it is and, as a result, the more likely they'll be to grant it. By approaching them early on you're showing you take them seriously, and you value them as potential members of your team.

Have this dialog in person and at the other party's office or home. That not only signals the importance you place on the process, but also clearly puts you in the position of supplicant. It's human nature to be more magnanimous when in a position of superiority, so the more humble you seem the better your chances. If it's with a family member, have it either on the weekend or during the evening. It should be at a time when you've the least chance to be interrupted.

Explain very clearly what you are planning to do, what you need from the other party, and how important they are to your success. Explain, with all the emotion and enthusiasm you can muster, you're asking for their help to fulfill your life-long dream. Acknowledge you're asking them to make a sacrifice. . . even if you're not. If your request is met with anger, simply absorb it and refuse to respond in kind. Instead, turn up the humility a notch and reiterate your respect and admiration. If consent is essential to your Second Act, grovel if need be. Don't let pride stand in the way of the life of your dreams.

Anticipate every possible objection and have a way to either eliminate or mitigate each. For example, if you're asking your

---

PAUL GAUGUIN

At the age of twenty-two, Paul Gauguin seemed set for a comfortable middle class life. He was happily married and just starting a promising career as a stockbroker. It was a remarkable turnaround for a young man with a turbulent childhood. Born in 1848, Gauguin and his parents left France and sailed for his mother's native Peru when he was only three years old. His father died on the voyage, and it took four years for his mother to be able to return with him to France. Gauguin attended a seminary but left at the age of seventeen to join the merchant marine. But by 1870 he was established in his brokerage and

---

spouse to pick up the slack financially while you go back to school, you could offer to repay this sacrifice in kind for his or her own Second Act later, whatever it may entail. If that's not enough, offer to cut back on expenses benefitting you alone, or that typically are in your control. If you're asking a lender to extend the terms of a loan or allow you to temporarily suspend payments, you can offer a higher interest rate or an additional guarantor.

Be persistent and forthcoming. Probe for objections you may not have anticipated and look for ways to overcome them. One secret is to push for specific and tangible reasons for refusals. Once you have a reason, you can then address it directly. For instance, when prodded, a spouse might admit a fear you'll be tempted to be unfaithful if you go back to college and are surrounded by coeds. Ask what you can do to allay fears or concerns. Don't accept "nothing" for an answer. When you get an

outwardly seemed content. In 1874 he began painting on weekends and in 1876 one of his works was accepted into a prestigious show. His love of painting grew, and, encouraged by Camille Pissaro, he decided to launch a Second Act. At the age of thirty-five Gauguin gave up his career as a stockbroker to concentrate on his painting. He was soon separated from his wife and family and took up a Bohemian lifestyle that led him from France to Martinique to Panama, back to France where he shared a flat with van Gogh, and finally to the island of Tahiti. After a brief trip back to Europe he returned to Tahiti and then the Marquesas Islands. The one time stockbroker is today hailed as a forerunner of both surrealism and primitivism and a major influence on both German Expressionism and Picasso. ■

answer, agree immediately. The same holds true for less emotional objections. If an employer doesn't want to give his consent to your spending one afternoon a week at a college course, find out why. Perhaps he's worried your productivity will drop. Offer to more than make up for the time missed with additional hours.

In effect you're trying to find out the price you need to pay for the other person's consent and support. How high a price are you willing to pay to live the life of your dreams? In my experience, in cases where you are asking someone to make a financial, legal, or physical sacrifice, there's always a way to get the needed consent or support. In other words, everyone has their price. Ironically, it's only in cases where the support requested is emotional and psychological, rather than physical or financial, that I've witnessed outright refusals without rational reasons that could then be countered.

Exercise 1

Turn to a fresh page in your Second Act notebook and title it CONSENT REQUEST. As succinctly as possible, describe exactly what you are asking the other party to do. For example, "Take over evening child care while I attend classes," or "Do without vacations for three years in order to save money."

Next, try to come up with every possible response to your request. Give full rein to your imagination. Imagine the other party responding angrily, jealously, greedily, crudely, and in any other manner you can picture. Even if you think it unlikely your aunt who's a nun will get angry and curse, write the possibility down. The more potential responses you anticipate, the more prepared you can be, the more confident you'll feel, and the more likely you'll get the consent and support you want. Try to uncover a specific complaint behind even the most emotional possible response.

Finally, work up answers or responses to each possible reaction. Look for specific cures for specific complaints, rather than emotional responses to emotional outbursts. The secret will be to make the discussion as rational as possible.

Rewrite and refine the possible responses and your counters, over and over again, using scratch paper. Keep this rewriting process up until you can reduce each response and counter to a two or three word cue. For instance, "Unfair—Reciprocate after." Transfer this list of cues to a page in your Second Act notebook and commit them to memory by repeating them over and over like a mantra. When you have them all down cold, you're ready for the conversation.

If, despite all your efforts, you're unable to get nonessential consent, simply thank the other person for listening and go on with your Second Act. Living well is the best revenge, and you'll

---

Famous Second Act

RON HOWARD

Ron Howard began his acting career at the age of two, following in the footsteps of his parents, who were both actors. Howard had incredible success as a child actor, working in films like *The Music Man* and television programs. He became a fixture during an eight-year run on *The Andy Griffith Show*. As he grew older, Howard continued to land starring parts in films like *American Graffiti* and television series such as *Happy Days*. But through it all, he was working on his Second Act: writing and directing. At the age of fifteen Howard won a Kodak-sponsored contest for short films. In 1977, at the age of twenty-three, he cowrote and directed *Grand Theft Auto*. In 1982 he officially began his Second Act, leaving *Happy Days,* and directing *Nightshift,* which became a hit. That was followed with other directing hits including *Splash, Cocoon, Backdraft, Apollo 13,* and *How The Grinch Stole Christmas.* In 2002 Howard's Second Act was topped by winning the best director's Oscar for *A Beautiful Mind.* ∎

---

soon be living better than ever before. But if, after using all the techniques I've outlined, you're unable to win consent and support that's essential to your Second Act, you've reached a crossroads.

Almost certainly, this refusal is based on emotion rather than logic, because you've expressed your willingness to do anything and everything to win the other party's support. You must decide whether, despite your previous calculations, you can launch your

Second Act without their backing. I don't believe you should let someone capriciously keep you from living the life of your dreams. And if you've reached this point, the objection can only be capricious. I simply can't understand how someone, particularly a loved one, could ever do such a thing when they hear it framed in these terms. How can someone not in fact do everything in their power to help a person they love be happy, especially when all their possible material or logistical concerns have been answered? Still, I've seen it happen. Some people are so insecure they can't stand others to have something they lack, even if it's something as basic as happiness. When facing this dilemma you must ask yourself what is more important: maintaining your relationship with a person who doesn't want you to be happy, or living the life of your dreams?

CHAPTER 10

Education and Training: What's in a Name?

"Nature is more powerful than education; time will develop everything."
—BENJAMIN DISRAELI

The importance of formal education and training is overrated. Perhaps because, as a society, we are more than a century removed from the days when people primarily learned on the job, whether as a law clerk or an assistant auto mechanic, we've come to believe the only way to acquire knowledge and skills is in an organized classroom setting. Sure, the world has grown more complex, whether it's in human relations or technology. But that doesn't mean you need to get a degree in order to, let's say, manage a business.

Technical knowledge and proficiency can be, in fact, better learned on the job than in a classroom. Ask a teacher whether he or she learned more in an educational theory course at college or in their first semester standing in front of a room full of children. And theoretical understanding is probably acquired more easily in a less formal, more intimate setting. There's a reason Plato, Buddha, and Jesus all taught while relaxing outside.

I'm not saying a theoretical background and historical knowledge aren't helpful to launching your Second Act, only that they are not as important as practical experience.

Of course, that's going to be a tough sell in some cases. After all, most of those already in a profession or field will have acquired their knowledge in the traditional way. That means they're invested in the conventional approach. Someone who spent six years and tens of thousands of dollars getting their bachelor's and master's degrees in business isn't going to be so quick to admit those sheepskins aren't necessary. It takes a very secure and open-minded person to acknowledge the path they traveled isn't the only path. And while there are such enlightened people out there, I don't think you can count on only coming into contact with them.

In other cases, there may be no way around the need for an extended period of education and training. For example, you cannot become a doctor without graduating medical school and then passing a series of rigorous licensing examinations. If your Second Act truly does require formal education and training, you need to factor the time and money involved into your calculations about whether money and duration are obstacles.

But if you're entering a field without such strict qualifications, what's most important is *you* understand you may not need the education and training you assume is a requirement. For instance, a degree from the Columbia University School of Journalism, or any degree for that matter, isn't needed to be a newspaper reporter. What you need is the skill to practice in whatever field you're entering. How you get that skill is less important than that you have it. Having internalized that notion, you can then focus on getting the minimum formal credentials you need to show that you've "gotten your ticket stamped." That might mean working as an intern, or getting a professional certificate, or a degree from a college that specializes in distance learning.

Famous Second Act

GLENDA JACKSON

Classically trained actress Glenda Jackson left the Royal Shakespeare Company for success in Hollywood, winning Oscars in 1969 for *Women in Love* and in 1973 for *A Touch of Class.* Working on both the stage and in film, Jackson's career was marked by her portrayals of complex women, notably Queen Elizabeth I and the poet Stevie Smith. Involved in the labor movement throughout her career, Jackson raised the curtain on a Second Act in 1992 when she was elected to Parliament and devoted herself full time to politics. In 1997 she was appointed Transport Minister in Tony Blair's government. ■

Would you be better off with a degree from Harvard than with one from Phoenix University? Actually, I don't think so. First, it would cost you far more money. Second, it would probably take you more time. And third, it would play against your strengths. Let's face it: Since you're launching a Second Act you are automatically different from the majority of others with whom you'll be competing. No amount of backtracking and then following a traditional path is going to disguise the fact you're different. Instead, embrace and highlight your uniqueness—that's what will make you a superior candidate.

But before you sign up for those online classes, make sure you actually need the credential you're pursuing.

Exercise 1

If you believe you lack the education or training to succeed in a particular Second Act, but aren't sure, you need to do some research.

The individuals, organizations, and institutions that provide education and training do an excellent job of marketing their indispensability. In some cases they've led the public to believe it's an objective impossibility to do something without their course or lessons. Similarly, individuals who are already doing what you'd like to do in your Second Act may have a vested psychological interest in promoting the same path they took. That's why your research must be targeted at unbiased authorities.

1. *Contact reference librarians.* Telephone the central public library in your area, or the nearest university library. Ask to speak to someone in the reference department. Explain that you're looking to research on careers in the area of your Second Act. Ask whether there is either a branch library that specializes in holdings for that area, or whether there is a particular reference librarian with that expertise. Make an appointment with the relevant librarian. That will ensure you get far more time and attention than if you just walk in cold. At the library, explain that you're looking for information on the actual, rather than perceived, requirements for the area in question. The librarian will be able to point you in the right direction. Keep your notes in your Second Act notebook.

2. *Contact government agencies.* Telephone the office of your local member of Congress. Begin by saying you're a constituent and giving your name and address. Then, ask for help in finding out which federal, state, and local agencies or bureaus govern the field or industry you're

exploring. Write the information down in your Second Act notebook. Rather than doing an online search, telephone the public information office of the agency or bureau. Start your conversation by saying you're calling on your Congressional representative's recommendation, using his or her name. Ask for the name and direct contact telephone number of the person with whom you're speaking. Then, explain exactly what information you're looking for. Note you're concerned with the actual, rather than perceived requirements for a particular field or credential. Take comprehensive notes.

If you discover your fears of lacking required education or training were wrong, you can focus on getting the minimal background you need to be able to sell yourself. That can be accomplished by getting some hands-on experience.

If you discover your worries about not having sufficient education and training were justified, you need to do whatever you must to get your credentials. There may be some ways to speed up the process, however.

GET SOME HANDS-ON EXPERIENCE

Once you move past the actual physical production of a product or service, there is a remarkable sameness to most industries and professions. That's because the fundamentals of management, marketing, and finance don't change when you move from the consumer electronics business to the children's clothing industry. People interact and communicate the same whether they're working in a dentist's office or for a professional football team. If you understand the key in capitalism is to generate profits, then you've already most of what you need to know to succeed in business. And if you realize the key to dealing with people is to

JIMMY CARTER

Few Americans have had as remarkable a reversal in their Second Acts as James Earl Carter, 39th president of the United States. Born in 1924 into a devout Baptist family, Jimmy Carter was always interested in world affairs. He graduated from the U.S. Naval Academy in 1946 and served for seven years, specializing in nuclear engineering and rising to the rank of lieutenant commander. Upon returning home to Plains, Georgia, Carter married and took over the family's peanut farm and business. His interest in community affairs led to a successful run for state senator in 1962. In 1971 he was elected governor. In 1976 his meteoric political career brought him the

provide or elicit clear goals, work hard to meet them, and along the way treat everyone with respect, you're prepared for any work dealing with people.

So what really does separate, say, the aerospace industry from the furniture business? Jargon and industry norms. The rest of the education and training you need can come from the school of hard knocks.

Selling the relevance of your experience from another field, and the added value you provide by offering a fresh approach, will be much easier if you demonstrate respect for your new industry or field. You can do that by having just enough education to know the vocabulary and traditions. There are three quick and simple ways of acquiring that kind of information, short of going back to school:

Democratic nomination for the presidency, which he won in a very close election over the incumbent, Gerald Ford. His notable achievements—including the Panama Treaty and the Camp David Accords between Israel and Egypt—were overshadowed by the Iranian Hostage Crisis. In 1980 he lost in his re-election bid by one of the largest margins in history. But what some would view as failure, Carter saw as a chance to launch a Second Act. Selling the family farm and business to pay off their campaign debts, the Carters raised funds to build a conflict resolution center, which has to date worked in more than 65 countries. Carter himself has been active in efforts to promote peace and democracy in ravaged areas such as Ethiopia, Somalia, Haiti, and the Middle East. In 2002, Carter was awarded the Nobel Peace Prize. ■

1. *Sign up for an apprentice program.* Contact larger employers, professional associations, and government employment offices to find out whether there are any apprentice programs in the field you're entering. Interested in a new career in the theater? Find out if there are apprentice programs at any nearby regional theaters or nonprofit touring theater groups. Don't limit yourself to formal apprentice programs. You can create your own where none exists. For instance, if you want to become a cabinet maker, see whether there are any finish carpenters in your area who wouldn't be future competitors and are willing to hire you as an assistant. If you're older than the typical age of most apprentices don't worry. You aren't the only individual who's launching a Second Act. By 2010, apprentices typically will be middle aged or seniors.

2. *Apply for an internship.* That same age shift is also taking place in the world of internships. Apprenticeships, by their nature, offer more practical training than internships. But in some fields it may be enough to spend six months hanging around an office, filing and making copies, if it gives you the chance to learn the language and culture. By law, candidates for internships cannot be discriminated against because of age. And in fact, the trend today is for companies to grab interns with experience in other areas. Organizations look on these experimenters or career shifters as providing added value and being capable of contributing far more than a junior in college.

3. *Take an entry-level job.* If there are no formal opportunities for apprenticeships or internships in the area you're pursuing, look for an entry-level position. Let's say you're a school teacher, but your dream is to be a magazine editor. Look for entry-level opportunities at publications. If your age or experience becomes an issue, explain you're launching a Second Act and are willing to start at square one. Stress how much more you can provide than someone who is fresh out of school. If you're questioned about a time commitment, note that, because you're mature and are actually looking to learn, you'll be likely to stay in the position longer than someone whose only concern is to get material for their resume.

Exercise 2

Head a fresh page in your Second Act notebook HANDS ON EXPERIENCE. Write up a list of all the expert sources on the area of your Second Act whom you've come across in your previous exercises. This can include mentors already in the field, reference librarians, contacts at trade or industry associations, and any resource you've found valuable. Contact each source and explain you're looking for apprenticeship programs, internships, or entry-level jobs that could give you a taste for the field. Stress your goal at this point is knowledge, not money. Compile a list of any leads. Apply for each and every opportunity you discover, choosing the one that offers you the best opportunity to get a quick, thorough education in the field's jargon and culture. Don't worry about whether or not it offers a chance for future growth. This is a learning experience, nothing more.

SHORTCUTS TO CREDENTIALS

If in your Second Act you're entering a field or profession that requires a certain education and training, hands-on experience won't be enough. That doesn't mean, however, there aren't short-cuts available to cut the cost and shorten the duration of the education and training. Here are four possibilities:

1. *Study while you work.* In some industries programs have been established that let you begin working at your chosen profession while you're still acquiring needed credentials. Generally all that's necessary is for you to complete an intensive crash course and to enroll and then eventually pass the required classes. In fields and regions where there's a shortage of personnel, such as inner city school teachers, tuition may even be waived or picked up by the employer.

2. *Study part time.* If you're unable to devote full time to acquiring the education and training you need for your Second Act, you can study part time. Most educational institutions are expanding evening, weekend, and summer offerings in response to the demands of older and return-ing students. If money is an obstacle, part-time study of

your new field can be coupled with continued full-time work in your old field. If money is less of an obstacle but still an issue, part-time study could be combined with efforts to get hands-on experience in the new field, such as with an entry-level job.

3. *Get a certificate.* If you already have some academic credentials, but they're not in the area mandated by your new field, you don't necessarily need to get a second bachelor's degree, or a master's degree. Many colleges have certificate programs that offer a formal credential for intensive study in a specific area. Because these programs are designed for the professional advancement of returning students, they can be very flexible. It may be possible for you to, for instance, get a certificate in corporate finance, rather than return to school for a complete MBA. The time and money savings can be substantial.

4. *Study online.* Distance learning is in the process of revolutionizing American education. While earning a degree online will still require a considerable time commitment on your part, the cost will be far lower than if you were a traditional student. In addition, you can fit lectures and coursework into your schedule, making it possible to both go to school and work full time. Major universities are expanding their distance learning programs. There are also a number of fully accredited institutions that specialize in distance learning.

Exercise 3

Contact the reference department at the largest library in your area. Ask to speak to a librarian who specializes in education. Make an appointment to meet with him or her. Similarly, call the alumni office of your alma mater and ask for the name of an academic counselor experienced in working with returning students. Again, make an appointment to either meet or speak on the telephone. Turn to a fresh page in your Second Acts notebook and title it EDUCATION SHORTCUTS. Write down the names and contact information of the people you'll be meeting. Then, develop a list of your educational needs. If, for instance, you need to demonstrate a proficiency in a foreign language, note that. Include your personal needs, too. That could mean you need to be able to take classes online or in the evening. Any financial obstacles should be duly noted as well. When you meet or speak with your sources, explain what you're trying to do in your Second Act. Ask them for help in finding flexible educational options. Obviously, take copious notes.

To a large extent, the need for education and training isn't itself an obstacle, but the cause of other obstacles, particularly money and duration. You'll have greater success at trying to mitigate, rather than working to eliminate, education and training obstacles. Do all you can to minimize how much education and training you need or to discover shortcuts. Then, spend the bulk of your time working at eliminating any resulting money and duration obstacles.

CHAPTER 11

Timing and Location:
Take Charge of Your Success

"There never is but one opportunity of a kind."

—HENRY DAVID THOREAU

I've grouped these two obstacles together because I believe most of the problems people have with them come from their view of success. Let me explain.

Do you believe there's a best time for you to launch your Second Act? Maybe you're an advertising executive with a working spouse and two children in high school. Your dream is to go to cooking school and eventually start your own catering business. But you're hesitant because you don't think now is the right time. You're waiting for the stars to all line up perfectly. You think that will happen in six years, when both your children will be out of college and your spouse will be ready for retirement.

Perhaps you think there's only one place from which you can start your new life. It could be that you're a school teacher living in Atlanta whose dream is to act. You think you can't achieve your Second Act without moving to either New York or Los Angeles because those are the only places where actors can hone their craft and become noticed. You're divorced and share custody of your children, making a move problematic.

Both reactions sound reasonable and mature. But if you take this approach to your Second Act, you'll probably never succeed. Why? Because you're not taking responsibility for your own success.

THERE ARE BETTER, BUT NO BEST TIMES

Thinking the timing isn't right for launching a Second Act is very common. . . and it's always an internal rather than external barrier. Yes, there could be better times than the present to change your life. Perhaps it would be easier to make a transition when your children are out of college. Maybe things will be smoother financially if you wait for the stock market to rebound before you start a new business. It seems to make sense to wait for the best possible moment to launch your Second Act.

But that moment doesn't exist. There is no best moment. Yes, there may be better times. In fact, there will always be better times. . . and that's the problem. If you're waiting for your kids to graduate college, why not wait for them to get jobs, or to get their own apartments, or to get married, or to buy their own house, or to have their own kids? Waiting for the market to rise sounds like a good idea. How high must it get for it to be high enough? The market could always go higher and that would make your Second Act even easier. And, if it has a setback while you're waiting, well, it will bounce back again.

Exercise 1

Turn to a fresh page in your Second Act notebook and title it PERFECT MOMENT. Write down what you're counting on happening that will make some moment in the future a better time to launch your Second Act. Maybe you've decided it will be less trouble to shift careers until after your spouse finishes his or her education. Imagine that you've reached that point. Is there something else that could take place to make your circumstances better? Having waited for your spouse to finish his or her education, why not then wait for him or her to get a job. Write that down under your initial observation. Once again, project forward to a time when both your hoped for events have taken place. Is there yet another event that could transpire to make your Second Act easier? Maybe you'd be better off if you wait for your spouse to get a raise. Note that as well. Continue listing improvements—a promotion for your spouse, his or her job transfer to a more conducive location, his or her retirement—until you (a) accept there will never be a perfect time; (b) realize you could be dead before all this happens; or (c) run out of room on the page.

Obviously, I'm being a bit of a wise guy. But my point is a serious one: Things can always get better. While usually that's good news, in this case it's a problem. If you start waiting for a better time, you're apt to keep on waiting. Wait on the possibility of improved circumstances, and you'll wait forever. It's like trying to time the stock market. Why sell now when the price could get higher, you might ask yourself. Or, you could think there's no point in buying now since the price could drop. There will always be better times to launch your Second Act. But there will never be a best time to do it, and there is never a bad time to follow your dream. Just look at the story of Ray Kroc who tried, again and again, to launch his Second Act.

By all means do what you reasonably can to make raising the curtain as easy and painless as possible. If that means waiting until you get your year-end bonus before quitting your job, or delaying a relocation until your sixteen year old goes away to college, that's fine. Just don't look for a perfect moment. At some point, in order to launch your Second Act and live the life of your dreams, you need to step out from the wings. Sure it's a risk when you finally hit your mark and the stage lights go up. But if you don't take that risk, you lose your chance at happiness.

We all know of people who have been waiting for a perfect opportunity to come around, and who have, in the process, frittered away their lives. It might be the graying bachelor, always waiting for the perfect woman, who now feels love has passed him by. It could be the ambitious coworker whose always been waiting for the right time to strike out on her own but never has. I don't want you to be someone who is always waiting for your "real life" to begin. I want you to live that dream life.

CHANGE IS GOOD, NOT BAD. . .

If you've listed location as an internal barrier to your Second Act that means you've determined you're able to move to a different location if, in fact, it is vital, but you're hesitant. If the move is possible, what are you really worried about? A shift in location and all the planning, arranging, and grunt work it entails, isn't fun. It can be hard uprooting your life and starting over in a new place. But not so hard that it should keep you from living the life of your dreams.

In my experience, if a change in location is called for and moving is possible, the only thing that ever holds people up is fear of change. Change isn't bad. Changing from being unhappy with your life to being happy with your life is good. If you must go through a bit of a headache and some temporary loneliness or feeling of displacement, that's okay. As I wrote earlier, I never said your Second Act would be painless or easy. If it were, you would have done it a long time ago. You cannot expect to climb a mountain without getting tired and working hard. You can't expect to launch a Second Act without some sacrifices.

Famous Second Act

RAY KROC

Ray Kroc didn't even settle into his first act until he was thirty-five years old. Born in Oak Park, Illinois, in 1902, Kroc led a peripatetic life. Lying about his age, the fifteen-year-old Kroc became an ambulance driver in World War I. Returning from Europe he got a job selling paper cups for the Lily Tulip Company. Obviously still searching, Kroc took work as a jazz pianist and then moved to Florida to cash in on its 1920s real estate boom. None of these efforts panned out, so by 1926 he was back working for Lily Tulip where he settled down. But in 1937 he invested his life savings to purchase the exclusive marketing rights to the "Multimixer," a five-spindle commercial drink mixer. For seventeen years he traveled America selling the machine. Then, in

I'm not counting on you to embrace a life of constant change and reinvention. (Although that would be wonderful, and, as you'll read later, that's exactly what I've done.) I'm just hoping, having realized your internal location barrier is just some residual fear of change, you're ready to set it aside and move on. If you can't, if you're unwilling to at least accept change, you'll never have a Second Act.

. . .BUT IT DOESN'T NEED TO COME ALL AT ONCE

If you've determined a specific location, different from where you are today, is absolutely essential to your Second Act—say your

1954, stunned by an order for eight of the giant mixers by Mac and Dick McDonald, the owners of a couple of small San Bernadino, California, burger and shake shops, Kroc paid them a visit. Inspired by their business of offering a limited menu of inexpensive items in a fast, assembly-line fashion, Kroc saw potential and the chance for a Second Act. He negotiated a deal with the McDonald brothers, giving them 0.5 percent of the gross in exchange for unlimited use of their name and concept. Kroc opened his first McDonald's restaurant in Des Plaines, Illinois, in April, 1955. Within six years, there were more than 130 McDonald's across the country. In 1961 Kroc bought out the McDonald brothers for $2.7 million. At the time of Kroc's death in 1984 there were more than 7,500 McDonald's restaurants across the world with annual sales of more than $8 billion. ■

dream is to work on a deep sea salvage team but you live in Oklahoma—you need to move. Unfortunately, that's sometimes far more difficult to actually do than to suggest. Despite the advances in information technology and telecommunications, roots still run deep. Spouses and children have their own links to a community. That's why I usually suggest a gradual relocation if moving is problematic.

Start off by going to your new location on weekends, or for a couple of weeks at a time. I know that can create problems of its own by increasing the cost and duration of your Second Act. Still, I think it's better, and easier, to save or raise the extra funds needed or find other ways to cut back on the time required, than it is force a difficult and rapid relocation on your family. I like to compare it to cultivating strawberries: A gardener lets the new shoots form roots of their own, before cutting them off from the mother plant. Give yourself and your family time to form new roots in your new community before cutting yourself off from your previous home.

IT MAY BE A BETTER LOCATION, BUT NOT AN ESSENTIAL ONE

You might be disappointed I only offered one possible solution to the location barrier. But that's because I think it's actually a very rare obstacle. Most often, people think relocation is necessary when it really isn't. Just as with timing, there may be better locations to launch new careers, but that doesn't mean your current location makes it impossible for you to succeed.

Exercise 2

Telephone the central public library in your area, or the nearest university library. Ask to speak to someone in the reference department. Explain you're looking to do research on individuals who've done whatever it is you're planning on doing. Ask whether there is either a branch library that specializes in holdings for that area, or whether there is a particular reference librarian with that expertise. Make an appointment with the relevant librarian. That will ensure you get far more time and attention than if you just walk in cold. Set aside one weekend day to do some empowering research. At the library, explain that you're looking for brief biographical sketches of people who succeeded at the field you're pursuing. Add you're specifically looking for information on where these individuals began their careers or professions. Odds are the librarian will be able to provide you with some reference volumes or with links to a number of databases. Spend some time leafing through the pages or browsing the onscreen entries. Label a fresh page in your Second Act notebook LOCATION REBELS. Make a note of every individual you discover who began his or her path to success from somewhere other than the conventional location. Stop in time for dinner or when you've filled more than three pages. Make copies of any entries you find particularly inspiring and tuck them into your notebook. Add your name to the list. Read the names over and over until it sinks in that you don't necessarily need to move to succeed.

I'm not denying there may be more opportunities to, let's say, become an actor if you're in New York or Los Angeles. But that doesn't mean you can't become successful starting out somewhere else. Look at John Mahoney who launched his Second Act as an actor out of Chicago. Just because a certain region is primarily associated with an industry or field, doesn't mean it has a monopoly on success in that area. In popular music, for example, hit acts have come from previously unrecognized regions: REM and the B52s came out of Athens, Georgia, in the 1980s, not New York; Pearl Jam and Nirvana put previously ignored Seattle on the West Coast music map.

Why not launch your Second Act in your current location? Travel down the road to success in your hometown for as long as you can. If at some point you discover you can go no further without moving, then relocate. You'll have the advantage of a firmer foundation and more experience, which will speed your success in your next location. You'll also have demonstrated dedication and aptitude, which will make it easier for you to sell the rest of your family on a part-time and eventually a full-time relocation.

Odds are you can at least get started on the road to success from where you are today. It may not be easy, but nothing worth doing is ever easy. It could be an uphill climb, but getting to a summit is an uphill climb. You can do this, if you want it badly enough.

Famous Second Act

JOHN MAHONEY

Born and raised in Manchester, England, one of the first things nineteen-year-old John Mahoney did when he moved to the United States was to join the Army and work on losing his accent. Leaving the military, Mahoney started an academic career, earning a bachelor's degree from Quincy College and then a master's in English from Western Illinois University. He eventually established himself as an editor of medical trade publications for doctors and college professors. At the age of thirty-seven, returning to a childhood passion, Mahoney decided to take classes at the St. Nicholas Theater in Chicago, founded by playwright David Mamet. Encouraged by Mamet and a classmate, John Malkovich, Mahoney quit his job and started his Second Act, joining Chicago's Steppenwolf Theater Company. He appeared in more than thirty Steppenwolf productions, as well as on- and off-Broadway, winning a Tony for his performance in *House of Blue Leaves*. In the 1980s he began landing film work including roles in *Tin Men* and *Moonstruck*. In 1993 he landed the television role as the retired policeman father of Fraiser Crane in the series *Fraiser*. ■

Early in this chapter I wrote about taking responsibility for your own success. Let me explain. There might be a better time than the present, but you can succeed by starting today. There may be a better place than where you are right now, but you probably can succeed from where you are. Your circumstances will never be perfect. If you're looking for an excuse or a reason to give up, this lack of perfection gives you an opportunity to blame inaction or surrender on forces outside yourself, "I could have been a successful songwriter if only I'd been able to move to Nashville;" "I could have hit it big with my idea for a mobile office park, if only I hadn't had to put Junior through college when the market was hot." It's easy to shift the burden of responsibility onto other people or other things. It lets you feel good about yourself and keeps you from having to make yourself vulnerable, "If I don't try, I can't fail."

But actually, if you don't try you automatically fail. If you try, you'll succeed. Take responsibility for your own success, rather than giving others the responsibility for your failure. It was Thomas Edison who said that genius was 1 percent inspiration and 99 percent perspiration. The formula is the same for success. By working your way through this book, by confronting the obstacles in your path, and by working to open the closed doors keeping you from the life of your dreams, you've demonstrated to me you have what it takes. Of all people, I think it was silent Calvin Coolidge who said it best, "Nothing in the world can take the place of Persistence. Talent will not; nothing is more common than unsuccessful men with talent. Genius will not; unrewarded genius is almost a proverb. Education will not; the world is full of educated derelicts. Persistence and Determination alone are omnipotent. The slogan 'Press On,' has solved and will always solve the problems of the human race." If you're willing to take responsibility for your own success, to take charge of your Second Act, to press on, you can succeed whatever your location.

CHAPTER 12

Esteem, Fear of Success, Fear of Failure, and Fatalism: Stop Being Your Own Worst Enemy

"Self-esteem creates natural highs. Knowing that you're lovable helps you to love more. Knowing that you're important helps you to make a difference to others. Knowing that you are capable empowers you to create more. Knowing that you're valuable and that you have a special place in the universe is a serene spiritual joy in itself."

—LOUISE HART

Because you've turned to this chapter I think I'm safe in assuming you're your own worst enemy. You are doing things to yourself you'd never let someone else do to you. You're belittling your own efforts and abilities with a vehemence you'd find intolerable if it came from others. Think I'm being too harsh? Maybe I am. But as a life coach I find the closed doors this chapter addresses to be the most frustrating to deal with in helping people launch their Second Acts. That's because they're all self-generated.

I'm not saying you're responsible for, as an example, your own lack of self esteem. The blame for that, or any other of these self-generated obstacles, could be placed on a number of factors. I'm neither a psychotherapist, nor in direct touch with you, so there's no way I could even guess why, for instance, you care so much about what others think. I'm calling these barriers self generated because you're choosing to keep them in place. You are the one continuing to invest power in, let's say, comments made by an ignorant high school teacher. You are the one continuing to think you're doomed to endlessly repeat a childhood failure. My frustration comes from seeing someone like you—someone who is ready, willing, and able to live the life of his or her dreams—never begin, or give up on, the quest because of psychological or emotional baggage. I also must admit, some of my frustration comes from my not having many tools for helping you overcome these barriers.

I don't have the kind of therapeutic training it takes to get some people past deeply ingrained problems. It's also next to impossible, I think, to really address these kind of issues in a book. Sure, the words on these pages can be understanding, empathetic, reassuring, and empowering. But we're engaged in a one-sided conversation here, not a dialog. And, that limits what can be accomplished.

What I'm going to try to do in this chapter is to point out, as clearly as I can, the fallacies on which these obstacles are built. Hopefully, increased awareness is all you need to overcome these barriers in your head. . . at least long enough to get your Second Act launched. Like a shot of anesthetic, awareness can deaden the feelings long enough for the procedure to work. Then, even if the effects start to wear off, the inevitable successes and positive feelings that come from being on the path to your dream life will energize you and keep the momentum building.

"WHAT WILL PEOPLE THINK?"

Are you hesitant about pursuing your dream because of what you perceive people will think of you? Maybe you're afraid that your friends will laugh when you tell them you're quitting your job as a stockbroker to become a disk jockey. Perhaps you're frightened your family will be critical if you decide to have a baby, on your own, at age forty-two.

Rationally, you must know it's what you think of you, not what others think of you, that really matters. You will never truly be happy living the life others want you to live. As the author and teacher Shakti Gawain[29] once warned, "Every time you don't follow your inner guidance, you feel a loss of energy, loss of power, a sense of spiritual deadness." The way for your soul to bloom is for you to live the life you want to live. Your spirits will soar; your emotional, spiritual, psychological, and even physical health will improve. You will look better and you will feel better, internally and externally.

If someone truly cares about you, he or she will see the positive impact your Second Act has had, and whatever qualms may have been felt will be set aside and replaced with shared joy. If he or she can't do that—if the criticism continues despite your obvious happiness—then he or she doesn't really love you for who you are. All that's important to such a person is what you are, not who you are.

Exercise 1

If you're having a hard time ridding yourself of the fear of what others will think, try this. Turn to a blank page in your Second Act notebook and title it TRUE FRIEND. Divide the page into two columns. In the lefthand column list the names of ten friends

---

[29] Author of *Creative Visualization* and *Living in the Light*

Famous Second Act

STEVEN VAN ZANDT

After 25 years as a producer, songwriter, and performer, Steven Van Zandt had carved out a successful career in rock and roll. While best known as "Little Steven," guitarist with Bruce Springsteen and the E Street Band, Van Zandt had also produced a record (*Hearts of Stone* by Southside Johnny and the Asbury Jukes) named by *Rolling Stone* as one of the top 100 albums of the past twenty years and had a solo record (*Sun City*) named by *Rolling Stone* as one of the top 100 albums of the 1980s. But, through it all he had never appeared on the cover of the famous music magazine. That was until his Second Act. In 1999 Van Zandt finally made it to the cover in the incarnation of Silvio Dante, mobster and recurring character in HBO's critically acclaimed series, *The Sopranos*. ■

---

or close relatives. Skip a line between each name. In the righthand column, write each individual's profession—dentist, for instance—or a short description of their role in society—stay-at-home mom, for example—on the same line as their name. Now, go back through the list, but this time, cross out the profession or role listed, and beneath it, insert another one. It could be something that would be a logical transition—like from accountant to financial planner—or it could be something absurd—such as from attorney to circus clown. Once you've finished revising the list, ask yourself whether your feelings toward any of the individuals as people would be different if the imagined change actually took place. Would you love your old college roommate any less if he stopped being a doctor and became a juggler? Of course not. Then why are you afraid others' feelings about you could change?

Besides, anyone who picks and chooses friends, or who parcels out affection or attention, based on another's career or lifestyle, rather than on character, isn't worthy of being your friend. And, it pains me to say, any family member who would withhold love because of what you do or because of the life you lead, rather than who you are, isn't deserving of your love.

You have a choice. You can pursue the life of your dreams, or you can pursue the life of someone else's dreams. I believe if you follow a path others have chosen for you, rather than the one you want for yourself, you're guaranteed to be unhappy. Follow your own path, and you'll be happy. As Robert Louis Stevenson once said, "To know what you prefer instead of humbly saying 'Amen' to what the world tells you you ought to prefer, is to have kept your soul alive."

"I'M DOOMED TO FAIL."

Are you hesitant to launch a Second Act because you're afraid of failure and are convinced you'll fail in an effort to reinvent yourself? In order to deal with this barrier, you'll need to analyze why you think failure is inevitable.

Exercise 2

Write REASONS FOR FAILURE on top of a blank page in your Second Act notebook. Then, spell out exactly what the basis is for your pessimism. Have you failed often in the past? Write down up to ten times you perceive you've failed. Perhaps you just have a low opinion of your own skills and abilities. If that's the case, write down what you believe are your permanent failings. (I'm not going to feed your negativity by offering up any examples. You'll need to do your own dirty work.)

Go over the list and decide whether it's a past history of failure or a perceived lack of skill that primarily accounts for your sense of impending doom. (No, you can't pick both.) Once you've made a choice, tear this page out of your notebook, crumple it into a little ball, and then light it on fire.

If your fear of failure comes from a past history of failure, you're misreading the situation. If anything, past failures are a plus. Need proof? Look at Ulysses S. Grant. A failure in his first effort at a military career and then in numerous business efforts, he went on to become one of America's greatest generals and then President of the United States. The best way to learn, some say the only way, is through trial and error. We learn very little from our successes. Having a number of failures in your past simply means you've had the advantage of learning lots of life's lessons. You're seasoned and experienced; you're a battle-tested veteran in life. Obviously, the secret is to change how you perceive your past. Those aren't failures, they're tutorials. I always say it's okay to look back—just don't stare.

If your fear of failure comes from a distorted self appraisal, you're both the victim and perpetrator of one of the world's most heinous crimes: stealing your own chance at happiness. I wish I had some catchy bromide or secret incantation that would instantly turn your lifelong pessimism into optimism. I'm sorry. I don't have a magic bullet. All I can tell you is that if you don't get out of this jail you've built in your own head, you're dooming yourself to unhappiness. It's a self-fulfilling prophecy: You don't think you can succeed. . . and so you won't. I hope realizing this is enough to at least temporarily get you to put your pessimism aside. If it's not? Put this book down right now and go talk to a

Famous Second Act

U. S. GRANT

Sam Grant was a serial failure. A graduate of West Point, he had served well in the Mexican American War, and was commissioned a captain. Loneliness for his wife and son while stationed at remote outposts led him to drink heavily. He resigned from the Army in 1854 and was forced to borrow the money necessary to return home to St. Louis. He turned to farming without success. Realtor was his next profession, followed quickly by stints as a country engineer and customs house clerk. He failed at each. He ended up selling firewood on the streets of St. Louis to try to make ends meet. By 1861 the thirty-nine-year-old Grant was reduced to working as a clerk in his family's leather store in Galena, Ohio. At the outbreak of the Civil War, he

good therapist. Tell him or her I sent you, and you need to learn you can succeed. When you're ready to accept your own worth as a human being, come back to this chapter. I'll be waiting.

"EVEN IF I LAUNCH MY SECOND ACT I'LL STILL BE UNHAPPY."

Are you convinced if you successfully launch a Second Act, you'll just find yourself back where you are now: unhappy with your life? As I wrote earlier in this book, I suffered from this fear of success for most of my life. For years I thought this was a blessing. I looked at it as being responsible for my ambition and drive. But, whatever its role as a motivating factor, I now know it was a

offered his services to the Union Army. Eventually promoted to brigadier general, Grant launched successful assaults on Fort Henry and Fort Donelson ... and his Second Act. When the opposing general at Fort Donelson asked for an armistice, Grant insisted on "unconditional surrender." The press links the phrase to Grant's given names, Ulysses Simpson, and a legend was born. Grant rose to command the Union Army and led it to victory. His fame and appeal led him all the way to the White House, winning election in 1868 and re-election in 1872. Returning to private life, a series of bad investments led to bankruptcy in 1884. Dying of cancer and desperate to provide for his family, he finished his memoirs just before his death. The two-volume Personal Memoirs earned more than $450,000 for his family and is today considered one of the classics of military literature. ■

curse. I was never able to get any joy or satisfaction from my achievements. When I reached a goal, it was gone, and I needed to reach another. I never took pride in a job well done. I believed my accomplishments would inevitably disappear. Success never stuck to me. Even when people complimented me, I'd correct them. I never really owned any of my success.

My fear of success came from sensing my being loved was contingent on my being successful. I was always striving to win my mother's affection. After her death I found myself feeling, among other things, a lack of motivation that was totally out of character. With the help of a therapist I was able to figure out what was going on. He helped me realize I wasn't feeling motivated because I no longer had my mother to please. The effect of this realization was almost instantaneous. Soon I had my motivation back. I started enjoying the fruits of my efforts. I began graciously accepting compliments. I now own my success.

I hope, upon some reflection, you'll realize you don't need to try to please the person or persons whose approval you've always sought. Odds are you don't need to keep winning their love; it's permanent. It's just somewhere along the line you and they got your signals crossed. You mistook efforts at motivation for signs of conditional love. And if you didn't make a mistake? If they really are only offering conditional love? In that case you'll never be able to please them no matter what you do. So rather than banging your head against the wall in a futile effort to win the unwinnable, start doing things to please yourself.

Rather than spending the rest of your life being unable to enjoy your success, being incapable of accepting compliments, and being unable to enjoy accomplishments, give yourself permission to be happy. That's also a self-fulfilling prophecy.

"FUTURE HAPPINESS AND SUCCESS ISN'T IN MY CONTROL."

Do you feel it's useless to try to launch a Second Act because you're just a prisoner of fate? Maybe you think that you've no control over how your life turns out. Perhaps you believe God is like a great puppet master in the sky, determining who gets a parking ticket and who gets cancer.

This sort of fatalistic view of life is based, however obliquely, on a fundamental truth: We are all going to die. No one can change that. No matter how much we exercise, how healthfully we eat, and how often we go to the doctor, we are all mortal. Everyone dies. But not everyone lives. You may not be able to prevent your inevitable death, but you do have control over how you live the time that's given you, however short or long it may be. What matters in life is quality, not quantity.

Fatalism is paralyzing. People who believe they're not in control of their destiny can't launch Second Acts. In fact, they're just waiting for the final curtain. When you give control over your life and your happiness to forces outside of your power, you are existing, not living. You are going through the motions, playing out the time God has given you, waiting for the end.

It isn't hubris to believe you're in charge of your life. God has given you free will. Use it. Take control of your future. Go after happiness. Pursue success. Launch your Second Act, and you will live a full and joyous life, no matter its duration. Take a lesson from those who truly have come face to face with death. Most come back from the precipice determined to live their life to the fullest, to make every day count. Life is a gift. I believe God intended for us to use it.

If after reading this chapter you don't feel as though you're able to transcend whatever psychological barrier is standing between you and your Second Act, I'd suggest contacting a good psychotherapist. While simply realizing the root cause of my own fear of success was enough to get me through that closed door, I needed a therapist's help to delve into my psyche and my past to make the discovery.

I don't view psychotherapy as a panacea. But if therapy is what it takes to be able to lead the life of your dreams, so be it. Just factor the cost and time into your calculations. Remember: Your outside matches your inside. It will be very difficult for you to fully appreciate your Second Act and get all the joy and happiness from it you deserve, if you've unfinished inside business. Renovate the neighborhood inside your head, and you'll find it easier to renovate your outside world.

PART 3

OPENING NIGHT

"Desire, ask, believe, receive."

—STELLA TERRILL MANN

CHAPTER 13

Writing Your
Second Act Script

"I have always thought that one man of tolerable abilities may work great changes, and accomplish great affairs among mankind, if he first forms a good plan, and, cutting off all amusements or other employments that would divert his attention, make the execution of that same plan his sole study and business."

—BENJAMIN FRANKLIN

It bothers me that improvisation is valued above planning. Someone who spontaneously throws ingredients together is heralded as a wonderful instinctive cook, while someone else who selects a menu far in advance, shops ahead of time, and measures carefully is seen as less talented. To many, a person who inherits or marries great wealth, like Gloria Vanderbilt, is seen as fascinating and romantic, while another who deliberately works her way to the top, like Mary Kay, is seen as provincial and mundane. Perhaps on some level we prize improvisation because we think success without planning is more creative, or a sign of God's blessing, and that deliberate, premeditated actions are commonplace and crude.

Whatever the reasons, this bias against planning is a threat to the success of your Second Act.

Actually, it's a threat to your success in anything you do, not just your Second Act. I encourage people to develop plans for all their larger life and career projects. That's because I believe major accomplishments cannot come without planning. You can't start a business on a wish and a prayer. You'll never be able to buy a home on the spur of the moment. And, you certainly won't be able to reinvent yourself without developing and sticking to a plan, or a script.

Your Second Act script will be the final entry in your Second Act notebook. This summation of all your work will be a critical structure underlying your efforts at self revolution. It will itemize every step in the process, from beginning to end, spelling out what you need to do to succeed and also offering warnings of potential failure. This isn't a business plan, *per se*, although it can serve as the germ of a such a document if your Second Act involves launching a business. It's an outline of what you personally need to do in order to succeed. Coupled with your Second Act notebook, the two together will serve as guidebook, checklist, and motivator, outlining the path you need to follow, itemizing the tasks you need to complete, and providing constant reminders of your goal.

Drafting your Second Act script will force you to bring all the thinking you've been doing together in one cohesive document that leaves no questions unanswered. Luckily, you've already done all the preliminary work. The Second Act notebook you've been keeping throughout this process contains all the raw material you'll need to develop your Second Act script. Your script will be a distillation of the results of all the exercises you've completed.

As with your Second Act notebook, the exact form of your Second Act script is up to you. Personally, I prefer a paper document, but I'm not a child of the information age. I think it's best seen as the concluding portion of your Second Act notebook. I

Famous Second Act

MELINA MERCOURI

Melina Mercouri catapulted to international fame as a film actress in the 1960 production *Never on Sunday*. But her fame didn't save her from being exiled from her native Greece in 1967 for her political beliefs. While in exile she continued her film career, starring in British and American productions. On returning to Greece in 1974, after a change in government, she lifted the curtain on her Second Act, winning a seat in Parliament in 1977 and then being named Minister of Culture in 1981. ■

---

look on your notebook as the raw material and your script as the "executive summary." If you find an electronic file to be more convenient and effective, that's fine. What matters is it remains readily available for consultation.

The first page, or "scene," in your Second Act script is the MISSION STATEMENT you prepared. It is your goal, your target, the purest distillation of what you want your Second Act to accomplish. As such, it is the purpose of everything that follows in your script.

The second scene in your Second Act script should be the list of CLOSED DOORS you developed. These are the hurdles you need to overcome to get to the goal described in Scene 1. Rewrite them with the most problematic first and the remainder in descending order or difficulty.

Next should be a series of individual scenes for each of the Closed Doors you've listed. Head each scene with the name of the hurdles, MONEY, for instance, or DURATION. Then, in as concise

a manner as possible, list any relevant facts you've developed or
uncovered, as well as the steps you've determined you'll take in
order to overcome this obstacle. Go back and look over the
results of all the exercises you completed that deal with the particular obstacle to find the information.

Let's say money is one of your obstacles. The scene in your
Second Act script examining money would start with what you've
determined to be your monthly deficit or your transition reserve
deficit. Then it would move on to list the steps you're planning to
take to overcome your money hurdle. In this case they'd be found
on the pages in your Second Act notebook you've labeled
INCOME INCREASES and EXPENSE REDUCTIONS. Each of
these entries now becomes an item on a money to-do list. For
example, your money to-do list might consist of

- Ask boss for raise.

- Talk to grandmother about collecting inheritance early.

- Speak with alumni office about renting out house for graduation weekend.

- Investigate options for refinancing mortgage.

- Transfer credit card balances to lower-interest credit card.

- Talk to broker about trimming homeowners insurance coverage.

- Talk to broker about trimming auto insurance coverage.

- Contact tax certiorari firm about appealing property tax
  assessment.

You should end up with one scene for every one of the closed
doors you've identified, each containing a checklist of things you
plan to do to work past the particular obstacle.

Finally, your Second Act script should conclude with "credits," a list of advisors and resources who can help you during your Second Act. Go through your Second Act notebook and compile a list of those who effectively served on your FOCUS GROUP, people you identified as mentors or as sources of power you could leverage, and individuals you found to be particularly effective information sources. These might include a very savvy librarian, or someone who had previously gone through the same process as you're entering, who was very generous with their advice and counsel.

If you're feeling ambitious you can supplement your Second Act script with information or sketches about individuals, famous or known only to you, who've done what you're setting out to do.

Even though you've completed your Second Act notebook and have culled some information and lists from it for your script, don't ignore the earlier pages. Much of what you've gone through in the exercises can come in handy throughout the Second Act process. For example, if you complete all the items on your to-do list for overcoming a particular obstacle, let's say money, and you find you're still not home free, looking back through your Second Act notebook can provide you with added steps. For example, you can look for additional ways to reduce your deficits, say, adding a search for a part-time job or efforts to increase your unearned income.

Don't think of your Second Act script as being etched in stone. Like a business plan or a resume, this should be an organic document. If, for example, a new obstacle crops up along the way, a description of it and your checklist for overcoming it should be added to your script.

How do you use your script? It's quite simple. Having placed the scenes dealing with the closed doors you face in order of their difficulty, you turn to your most vexing obstacle and start working on the first item in your checklist. When you complete it, or need to wait on something, move to tackle the second item. When you finish the first checklist you'll have overcome your most problematic hurdle. With growing confidence, move on to your second obstacle and the tasks needed to overcome it. Keep on going until all the closed doors are open, and you're living the life of your dreams. If at any step along the way you need help, contact the individuals you've listed in your credits. If you need inspiration along the way, read the success stories you've included in the script.

If you find it impossible to complete any particular task, realize this predicts your own failure. But having this advanced warning lets you work around it. Let's say you planned on leveraging the power of your brother-in-law, a dean at a local university, in getting into a degree program. Before you can use his influence, he leaves academia and enters private industry. Rather than doing without this "shortcut" and risking failure, or giving up altogether, you can go back to the earlier exercises and choose another technique to use as a replacement.

Drafting and consulting an outline of how you're planning to reinvent your life may seem to be like taking what should be a romantic adventure and turning it into a prosaic project. I suppose it is. But I'd rather you turn it into a pedestrian enterprise and succeed, than keep it a visionary scheme and fail.

CHAPTER 14

The Goal. . . or Another Beginning

"The joy of life consists in the exercise of one's energies, continual growth, constant change, the enjoyment of every new experience. To stop means simply to die. The eternal mistake of mankind is to set up an attainable ideal."

—ALEISTER CROWLEY

Congratulations. Today is the first day of your new life. Pick up your Second Act script and start down the road to the life of your dreams. It's okay to be nervous. Everyone is when they first hit the stage. But you're ready. Your first act has been a dress rehearsal for this new adventure. You've incredible resources to draw on: all the knowledge and wisdom you've gained throughout your life. You've rationally worked your way through the whole process. All you need is to physically do what you've already sketched out in your head and on paper. You're prepared. You know there will be some closed doors blocking your path. But you also know you've tools and techniques to open them. The journey probably won't be painless or easy. Nothing of real value is obtained without sacrifice and hard work. When you get there, however, you'll experience a joy and satisfaction that will make it all worthwhile. The experience of succeeding at a Second Act is sublime.

However, it isn't permanent.

What was your dream when you were ten years old? Was that still your dream when you were twenty. . . or thirty? Unless you were an unusually precocious child, I'm sure your dream life changed at least once, if not more, as you grew up. The more we experience of the world, and the more we learn about ourselves, the more our dream lives come into focus. Usually, though not always, the iconic dreams of youth—firefighter, soldier, nurse—give way to dreams more in tune with individual needs, skills, and wants.

When I was a little boy I wanted to be a doctor. In high school my dream was to host a radio show. By the time I graduated law school and went out in the real world, my mature dream was to become a real estate entrepreneur. After my recovery from tuberculosis, my Second Act dream was to be a successful life coach. As I grew up my goals shifted and focused on what I was good at and what answered my most pressing needs.

Recently I discovered dreams don't stop changing even after you launch your Second Act. They may not shift as dramatically as when we are younger, but they definitely change.

A small number of people are, by their nature, peripatetic. They're happy only while in the process of "becoming." Whenever they achieve something, the goal loses its lustre. For these restless souls, the malleability of dreams isn't news. These vagabonds don't need help in launching Second Acts; they need help staying in any one place long enough to build a stable life.

Most people aren't so nomadic. They simply feel they haven't had the chance to pursue what would have made them happy. They feel their life is dull, dreary, or boring. They launch a Second Act to finally lead the life of their dreams. And, after some analysis and preparation and hard work, they're able to do just that.

Famous Second Act

JESSE VENTURA

When James Janos left the Navy in 1973 after serving in Vietnam he wasn't sure of what he wanted to do. After a brief stint working as a bodyguard in California, the twenty-four year old returned to his childhood hometown of Minneapolis and enrolled at a community college. He dropped out after the first year. But the devoted body builder was spotted by a local wrestling promoter and given a job as a "bad guy surfer type." After ten years on the pro wrestling circuit, Janos, now known as Jesse "the Body" Ventura, started working as a commentator and actor. In 1990, upset at what he considered to be the ineffective local government in his home of Brooklyn Park, Minnesota, and encouraged by his wife, Ventura launched a Second Act in politics: running for mayor as an independent candidate. The outspoken charismatic ex-wrestler won, upsetting an eighteen-year incumbent in the process. Ventura decided to run for governor of Minnesota as a Reform Party candidate in 1997. Once again, he proved his critics wrong, winning the governorship in November, 1998. ■

But the story doesn't always end there. I'm starting to see a handful of Second Act people who are coming back to me for help in launching third, and in some cases, fourth acts. Initially, I thought these clients were either restless souls or people who had misidentified their true callings. I was wrong. They're not peripatetic. Nor did they make a mistake in choosing their Second Act. They certainly didn't fail. Far from it. They succeeded so

---

MICHAEL JORDAN

No one has ever failed and succeeded in Second Acts more publicly than Michael Jordan. Jordan led the Chicago Bulls to three consecutive National Basketball Association championships and then abruptly retired at the age of thirty to launch a Second Act as a professional baseball player. Unable to progress past the minor league level, Jordan returned to the NBA and picked up where he laid off, leading the Bulls to another three consecutive championships. Once again, Jordan retired and started a Second Act, this time becoming part owner and president of basketball operations for the Washington Wizards. But after two years on the sidelines and being unable to bring credibility to the NBA franchise, Jordan shifted gears again, and returned to the court as a player in 2002. While his season ended early due to injury, Jordan showed he could still compete at a high level. At the time this book was written it wasn't clear what Second Act Jordan was ready to launch in 2003. ■

---

wildly, so beyond their hopes, that they now know they can go through the process again and address another or a new dream. I believe these folks represent the leading edge of a new phenomenon: lifelong reinvention.

In retrospect I should have seen this would be the inevitable result of making Second Acts easier and more acceptable. There is no reason why people's hopes and dreams should stop growing or changing at a certain age. With life spans stretching further than ever imagined, and with those added years representing an additional active decade rather than ten years of dotage, there's ample opportunity for individuals to have third, or even fourth acts in their lives. After, say, two decades of a first act and another two decades of a Second Act, developing a new dream and wanting to launch a third act doesn't mark you as a dilettante. It marks you as someone who is living life to its fullest.

There is nothing wrong with relaxing or taking time to smell the roses. But there's also nothing wrong—and actually a lot right—with continually reinventing yourself. The two aren't mutually exclusive. Third acts needn't be full-time jobs any more than Second Acts needed to revolve around career or employment. Your third or fourth act could be to spend all your time gardening and, quite literally, smelling the roses. By looking at life as a constant process of self reinvention, you can live a fuller life than you ever imagined possible. You can lead as many lives as you wish, all packed into one life span. Most important of all, you ensure that the focus of your life remains on your life, not your death.

That was a revelation that struck me the year before I began working on this book. The prior eighteen months had been a very difficult time for me. My younger brother lost a long fight with cancer. Shortly thereafter, my mother passed away as well. In addition to feeling emotionally drained I began to feel physically run down as well. One weekend I started experiencing shortness of breath. I went to the doctor the next week and was told I needed heart bypass surgery.

I had the surgery. Everything went very well, and I'm now fully recovered. In fact, I'm exercising more now than ever before. But my emotional recovery wasn't as quick. Coming so close on the heels of my brother's and mother's deaths, my bypass surgery raised issues of my own mortality. . . issues I hadn't dealt with at all since my bout with tuberculosis more than twenty years earlier. Back then I was under such financial pressure that I didn't have the time to really deal with my own mortality. Money was my obsession. But, with my family in a much better financial position today, I didn't have to worry about money. I began to focus a great deal on my emotional needs instead.

I began to re-examine all the time and effort I was putting into maintaining my own office. Why was I doing it? What was I trying to prove? And to whom? After speaking with trusted advisors, including my wife, Corky; my children, Michael, Lori, Tracy, and Dana; my coauthor, Mark Levine; and my first law partner, Manny Zimmer, I decided to give up my independent legal and consulting practice. I realized I was spending more time managing and worrying about the office itself than working with clients, which was what I enjoyed.

I became a partner in a Fifth Avenue law firm at the age of sixty-nine. Left without management responsibilities, I now spend almost all my time working with clients and on my writing projects.

This latest reinvention has been rejuvenating. I'm focusing and listening to my clients more intently than ever before because I'm not preoccupied with what is transpiring in the outer office. I believe I'm getting better at what I do. I feel I'm more empowering, inspiring, and reassuring.

I've learned an important lesson. I already knew, both first-hand and through my clients, that launching a Second Act and finally leading the life of your dreams could turn your life from black and white into technicolor; it could bring joy to an otherwise humdrum existence. But I hadn't realized embracing your ability to continually reinvent yourself through your entire life could result in a spiritual renaissance.

Today, even while I'm in the middle of my latest reinvention, I'm keeping my eyes and ears and heart open to other dreams if they present themselves. I'm sure I'll launch yet another act before I'm eighty.

No matter how psychologically and emotionally satisfying it is to launch a Second Act, at some point it naturally comes to an end. Granted, it's an incredibly gratifying conclusion because you've been able to lead the life of your dreams. But on some level it's a bittersweet achievement. You no longer feel the thrill and anticipation of the process itself; that heady mixture of excitement, anxiety, and anticipation that got your blood flowing and pulse quickening is gone.

If you're one of those peripatetic souls who can never stop moving, you'll instantly launch another quest, going after something new, anything new. For most of us, however, living the life of our dreams can be fulfilling for quite some time, perhaps for some, the rest of their lives. But since we continue to grow and change, our dreams grow and change too, and sometimes the seeds of a new dream life take root.

I'm suggesting you cultivate that new seedling and nurse it into another act for yourself. By remaining open to the possibility of continual reinvention, you can turn your life from a means to an end, however gratifying, to an end in itself. The good life ceases to be a goal you're striving after and becomes an everyday occurrence.

Make reinvention your lifestyle, and you'll stay young at heart no matter your chronological age. Give free rein to your dreams throughout your life, as often as they come, and your soul will soar to heights you've never dreamed possible. Launch Second Acts, third acts, fourth acts. . . as many acts as you can dream up. By expressing your hopes and wishes, and pursuing them for as long as you live, you'll experience a rare freedom, both materially and spiritually. Life will cease being a trip toward mortality and instead will become a never-ending journey. Keep on reinventing yourself, and death becomes nothing more significant than the period at the end of this sentence.

Index